YOUR FAITH / YOUR COMMITMENT / GOD'S CALL

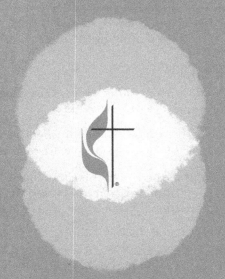

confirm.

TEACHING PLANS

APPROVED UNITED METHODIST CONFIRMATION

Confirm Teaching Plans
Your Faith. Your Commitment. God's Call.

Administrative Staff
Brian Milford, President and CEO, The United Methodist Publishing House
Marj Pon, Associate Publisher for Teaching and Learning

Editorial, Design, and Production Team
Jack Radcliffe, Lead Editor
Michael Novelli, Development Editor
Ben Howard, Associate Editor/Project Manager
Sheila K. Nimmo, Production Editing Supervisor
Keely Moore, Design Manager

Writers: Kevin Alton, Alisha Gordon, Nicholas VanHorn, Audrey Wilder, Ben Howard

Advisory Team: Dara Bell, Helene Foust, Brian Hull, David Johnson, Cindy Klick, DJ del Rosario, Kate Unruh

Reviewers: Rev. Justin Coleman, Jack Radcliffe, Rev. Lisa Beth White

16 17 18 19 20 21 22 23 24 25—10 9 8 7 6 5 4 3 2 1

MANUFACTURED IN THE UNITED STATES OF AMERICA

Contents

Meet the Confirm Team

Development Editor

Michael Novelli creates learner-centered resources and experiences for youth, children, and adults that explore the intersection of spiritual formation and experiential learning. Michael works as a content designer, church youth leader, and community advocate. He has a master of eductaion degree in integrated learning and is an adjunct instructor at North Park University, in Chicago. Michael and his family live in Elgin, Illinois.

Writers

Kevin Alton is a full-time youth ministry creative, particularly interested in the spiritual development of youth. Among other projects, he's the co-creator of Youthworker Circuit and is excited to be part of the grant team for Science for Youth Ministry. You can find him digitally as @thekevinalton. Kevin lives with his family near Chattanooga, Tennessee.

Alisha Gordon, M.Div., is the Executive for Spiritual Growth, United Methodist Women. She is a well sought-after writer, teacher, scholar activist, and public theologian with an interest in sharing the stories of the marginalized as a prophetic voice in the world. A native of Decatur, Georgia, Alisha holds a bachelor of English from Spelman College and a master of divinity from the Candler School of Theology at Emory University. Her unique blend of social commentary, religious engagement, and popular culture creates opportunities to use her faith and her social interests to engage in deeply meaningful conversations about race, difference, and social justice.

Ben Howard, Editor, Youth Ministry Partners, graduated from Oklahoma Christian University, with a degree in history and holds a master in theological studies from Lipscomb University. Prior to his work as an editor at Youth Ministry Partners, he served as a Christian Education Consultant with Cokesbury. He lives in Nashville, Tennessee.

Nicholas VanHorn has been a youth minister for nearly 15 years in both the United Methodist and Episcopal traditions. He graduated from Pfeiffer University, with degrees in youth ministry and Christian education,s and from Duke Divinity School, with a master in divinity. Nick resides with his family in Winston Salem, North Carolina, where he is the Director of Youth Ministries at St. Paul's Episcopal Church.

Audrey Wilder, Director of Christian Education and Young People's Ministries, Susquehanna Conference of The United Methodist Church. Audrey is a graduate of High Point University, with a degree in religion, and Duke Divinity School, with a master of divinity and a certificate in Christian education. Prior to her current appointment, she served as the Director of Youth Ministries at First United Methodist Church, in Hershey, Pennsylvania.

Advisory Team

Dara Bell, retired Conference Youth Coordinator, New Mexico Conference, The United Methodist Church

Helene Foust, Associate Director of Student Ministry, Indiana Conference, The United Methodist Church

Brian Hull, Assistant Professor of Youth Ministries, Asbury University

David Johnson, Associate Director, Texas Southern University Wesley Foundation

Cindy Klick, Youth Program Director, St. Andrew United Methodist Church, Highlands Ranch, Colorado

DJ del Rosario, Lead Pastor, Bothell United Methodist Church, Bothell, Washington

Kate Unruh, Ph.D., student and United Methodist Church researcher, Princeton Confirmation Project

Reviewers

Rev. Justin Coleman, Chief Ministry Officer, The United Methodist Publishing House

Jack Radcliffe, D.Min, Lead Editor, Youth Ministry Partners

Rev. Lisa Beth White, Ph.D. candidate, Boston University School of Theology

Introducing, Confirm!

Confirmation is a great responsibility, and it can be challenging. It's such an important time in the faith development of your students, and there's so much to cover, from theology to history to how the church works, and on and on. It can be overwhelming.

If you've taught confirmation before, you know this all too well; and if you haven't, you may feel a bit overwhelmed right now.

But we want you to know that we're here to help.

The *Confirm Teaching Plans* are designed to make sure you have all the information and guidance you need to make your time with your students as educational and affirming as it can possibly be. The lessons focus on the basic beliefs of a theologically sound, United Methodist faith; and each lesson contains creative, thought-provoking activities to help your students internalize what they've learned.

The teaching plans are also easy to follow because we want you to be able to focus your attention on the important part of confirmation, the students.

Too often, confirmation has been downgraded to the role of a checkpoint along the faith journey; but with *Confirm*, we want to provide you with the resources to reclaim confirmation as the first step on a journey toward a mature faith for your students.

This means that the time you spend with your students in the classroom is just the beginning of a conversation about what it means to be a Christian, living our your faith, your commitment, and God's call. With this in mind, *Confirm* embraces the importance of community in the journey of faith development and provides a number of resources in addition to these teaching plans that encourage the faith conversation beyond the classroom.

The Confirm Family of Resources

DIRECTOR GUIDE

This helpful guide provides direction for creating an effective discipleship path for teens using confirmation at your church. Complete with detailed instructions, the Director Guide help you integrate *Confirm* with the church's youth ministry program and other ministries throughout the church. In addition, you will be provided tools for creating specific confirmation assessments and reasonable expectations for youth, pastor, parents, and confirmation leaders.

STUDENT GUIDE

The *Confirm Student Guide* is integral to the process of immersing your students in the *Confirm* lessons. It provides innovative opportunities for reflection and creative expression during the lesson as well as resources and prompts for further exploration outside of the classroom. Through these activities, the Student Guide helps students grasp the lessons of *Confirm* in deep and meaningful ways.

DVD

The *Confirm DVD* includes 18 videos: 6 introductory videos and 12 white board videos.

Six videos by the Christian comedy group Blimey Cow serve to introduce the core themes of each unit in an energetic and fun way that gets students excited for the lessons to come.

The twelve white board videos are included in selected lessons to either deepen the lesson by explaining a challenging concept, such as sin or heaven, or to tell an important story, such as the history of the church or the story of Job. Each video is designed to be easily understandable without oversimplifying these important topics.

PARENT GUIDE

The *Confirm Parent Guide* provides an overview of confirmation and helps the parent and family establish their role in the process. The Parent Guide includes discussion starters, activities, and devotional suggestions for use at home. As teens prepare to take the vows of confirmation, they need to be surrounded by mature Christian adults who can love, guide, and nurture them. This love and nurturing begins at home, with the youth's parent or guardian.

MENTOR GUIDE

The *Confirm Mentor Guide* provides an overview of the confirmation process and equips mentors with suggested relationship-building ideas, as well as providing some of the dos and don'ts when taking on the role of mentor. A mentor doesn't need to be a trained theologian or someone who has all of the answers. Rather, a mentor is an adult who is mature in the faith and can walk alongside a young person the confirmation journey.

Unit 1: Our Journey

The confirmation journey is about equipping teens with the information, tools, and resources they need to make an informed decision about committing to follow Christ. The first step (these first four lessons) in that journey is helping your teens to understand the facets of Christian community. To that end, the first lesson of this journey is acclimating the teens with one another and their guides for the journey, namely their teachers and mentors. The subsequent two lessons will explore the importance of belonging and participation in the Christian community and challenge the teens to start practicing what it means to live in Christian community. The final lesson will connect teens with a Biblical understanding of belonging.

- CONTENTS -

Lesson

1 *Traveling Together*

LESSON DESCRIPTION: This lesson will acclimate all participants, teens, teachers, family members, and mentors to one another and to the concept of confirmation as a journey. Everyone should walk away with a better understanding of who is part of this confirmation community. While this lesson can be completed with only the involvement of the teens and teacher, it will be a greater experience of community development if family members and mentors participate as well.

Lesson Outline		
SECTION	**TOPIC**	**DURATION**
Connect	Community Survival	15 minutes
Explore	Exploring Emotions	20 minutes
Reflect	Documenting Emotions	5 minutes
Create	Dear Future Me	15 minutes
	Unit 1 video: "Our Journey"	5 minutes
Next	At home, at school, and in your community	Ideas to try this week

Supply List

Connect: Community Survival
- ❑ Survival items for each participant: pens, snacks, guide books, Bibles, and schedules and expectations)
- ❑ Copies of the Survival Chart (one copy for each person.)

Explore: Exploring Emotions
- ❑ 3 pieces of flip-chart paper or dry-erase board labeled "Samuel, Moses, I Feel"
- ❑ Sticky notes in 2 colors

Reflect: Documenting Emotions
- ❑ Student Guides
- ❑ Writing utensils

Create: Dear Future Me
- ❑ Student Guides
- ❑ Writing utensils
- ❑ Tape
- ❑ Unit 1 Video: "Our Journey"

Next
- ❑ Student Guides

Confirm Teaching Plans

- C O N N E C T -

Community Survival *15 minutes*

[**LEADER PREP:** All participants will be tasked with acquiring "survival" items necessary for our confirmation journey. Participants will gather these items by connecting through affinities (example: "Find three people with the same color hair as yours"); then you will ask a specific question (example: "What do you hope to learn from confirmation?").

Make copies of your specific schedule and expectations of participation for your class. For guidance on how to create this document, please refer to "Creating a Meaningful Confirmation Experience," in the Director Guide.

Make copies of the "Survival Chart" for each participant. Place on a table in the meeting space the survival items (pens, snacks, guide books, Bibles, and schedules and expectations). Participants will get all of these items at the close of the activity.]

SAY: Each journey requires certain elements in order to be successful. For some journeys, the supplies we pack are necessary for survival. Here is a list of supplies we need for our confirmation journey together.

[Give each person a copy of the "Survival Chart."]

SAY: There are seven important elements we will need. Let's read through them. Who'd be willing to take turns reading this out loud?

[Have students volunteer to read from the sheet the name of each item, its use, and how to get it.]

SAY: Do you understand? It will get a little loud and chaotic in here. That's OK! Let me give you a few tips before you begin. Now listen carefully:

1. You don't need to do these in order. You may start anywhere.

2. You don't need to gather people into groups. For example, for the first item, you need to find two people with shoes similar to yours. You may go to one person at a time. (However, that may take more time.)

3. You may ask the same person more than one question. But that is up to you to figure out. You are clever, and will come up with your own strategy.

4. **IMPORTANT:** Once you have gotten a response to the question, have the person who answered the question initial your chart.

SAY: After 12 minutes, we will see how many you were able to complete. Are you ready to get started?

Begin now.

> [Optional Wrap-Up: After time is up, gather together for a "pop quiz." Ask questions such as: Who of you can tell me the name of one person and his or her favorite salty food? Who of you can tell me the name of one person and the farthest place he or she has traveled? Who of you can tell me the name of someone and what he or she hopes to learn from confirmation?]

SAY: Great job! Who was able to get all of the elements? What was your strategy? What is something you learned about someone you didn't know?

> [Get some responses from participants.]

SAY: Take a moment to make sure you have all of the elements on this list. Many of them are on the table.

I hope that you had fun getting to know a little more about one another. Now, we are going to take some time to explore the kinds of emotions that might be associated with taking a journey.

- E X P L O R E -
Exploring Emotions 20 minutes

> [Divide a sheet of flip-chart paper or a dry-erase board into three sections: "Samuel," "Moses," and "I Feel." Assign half the participants into Team Samuel and the other half of the participants into Team Moses. If family members, mentors, and teachers are present, evenly distribute them between the two groups. Give each group a stack of sticky notes, with each group having a different color.]

SAY: At a quick glance, it is easy to think that the characters in the Bible are otherworldly. They do and say incredible things. Some of the characters almost don't seem human. But if we listen more carefully, we will notice that they aren't all that different from us. They thought and felt many of the same things you and I think and feel. Let's take a look at two characters in the Bible who, like us, were beginning an important journey. Before we read a part of Samuel's and Moses' stories, here is a little background about each of them. So settle in, focus your mind, and imagine these events as I read.

Samuel's journey with God began before he was even alive. Samuel's mom, Hannah, could not get pregnant. After years of infertility and ridicule, Hannah finally went before God and pleaded to have a son. She promised that if she had a son, she would dedicate his life to the service of God. God heard Hannah's plea, and Samuel was born to serve God. He lived the first couple of years with his family, but when he was still a young boy, Hannah brought him to be raised by the temple priest, Eli. You will pick up on Samuel's journey when he is still young, probably about your age or a little younger. Remember, he lived in the Jewish temple for many years, but he had never heard God speak.

Moses' journey with God also began before he was born. The Jewish people were living as slaves in Egypt. The power-hungry, insecure king of Egypt, Pharaoh, worried about a Jewish revolt, so he made a law that all Jewish male babies had to be killed. Moses' mother was Jewish. When she gave birth to him, she tried to save Moses by hiding him in a basket and floating him down a river. Miraculously, he was rescued by Pharaoh's daughter, who raised him in the palace as her son. The princess also brought in a Jewish servant to care for the baby ... little did she know, that servant was Moses' mother! (This sounds like a TV show, right?)

When Moses was an adult, he let his anger get out of control and he killed an Egyptian slave-driver. As a result, Moses became a fugitive and was hiding out in the desert living with a shepherd priest and his family. We are going to pick up on Moses' journey after he had been living in the desert for quite a while, and the old tyrannical Pharaoh had died.

Now, in groups, you will explore more about these characters. Here is how this will work:

Two volunteers will read the Bible verses aloud.

"Team Samuel" will read 1 Samuel 3:1-19; "Team Moses" will read Exodus 3:1-14 and 4:1-5, 10-16.

[Write these verses on the flip chart, dry-erase board, or on sticky notes.]

SAY: While you are listening to these verses being read, think about what the main character was feeling. Picture it in your mind.

After reading your passage, take the sticky notes you have been given and write all of the feelings and emotions you noticed from your character—either Samuel or Moses—one emotion per sticky note. Use as many sticky notes as you need to record all the different emotions and feelings in the passage. Post them on the board for your character.

You will have a little less than 5 minutes for this first portion of the exercise.

[After 5 minutes or when it seems like the groups are running out of things to write down, move on.]

SAY: Now that you've had some time to look at the emotions Samuel and Moses had on their journey, take a few minutes to record the different emotions *you* are feeling as you begin of this confirmation journey. Each person should come up with three or more sticky notes that honestly describe your own feelings.

Take the next 3 minutes to come up with these. Post them on the board in the "I Feel" area.

[Once the sticky notes are categorized, invite participants to point out any feelings on the Samuel and Moses boards that they think are surprising. Ask a volunteer from each group to read aloud the Scripture that had been assigned to the opposite group. Then, ask all the participants these questions.]

- What common feelings are we having about beginning this confirmation journey?
- What emotions did Samuel and Moses have that we also have? Why, do you think, did they feel some of the same feelings we do?
- How did Samuel and Moses respond to God?
- How might knowing about Samuel's and Moses' encounters with God prepare us for encountering God on our own journey?

SAY: One part of the confirmation journey is to ultimately accept personal responsibility for your relationship with God. For many people, that's a daunting and sometimes confusing process. During each lesson, you will have an opportunity to reflect on how what we are talking about affects your life, your faith, your relationships, and your decision to follow Christ. Most of your reflection will be done in your Student Guide. It will be the survival item that will help you keep track of what happens during this journey. We are going to start using this guide now to get us in the habit of reflecting on the things God is teaching us. Your first task will be to spend some intentional time reflecting on the emotions that you are bringing with you on this journey. Open your student guide and answer the questions there with honesty.

- R E F L E C T -
Documenting Emotions 5 minutes

Have the students write their responses to the following in their Student Guide:

- Be honest: How are you feeling about beginning confirmation? Write down three different emotions that you are feeling.
- Who from the Bible can you think of who experienced similar emotions before setting out on a journey with God?
- List 3 people you can talk to about your experiences and feelings during your confirmation journey.

- C R E A T E -
Dear Future Me 15 minutes

SAY: I need a volunteer to read the directions to the Create activity in the Student Guide.

[Ask the volunteer to read the directions.]

Discussion Questions As Time Allows
- What are you looking forward to most about confirmation?
- What intimidates you most about confirmation?
- Confirmation can be described as a journey, starting at one place and setting out on adventure to another place. What other metaphors would you use to describe confirmation?

SAY: We've spent a lot of time today considering many of the different aspects and emotions associated with going on a journey. Taking stock of where we are as we begin this confirmation journey will be important for helping us to see how far we've come when we reach the end of our journey. Now let's watch this short video to give us an idea of what we can expect during this first portion of our journey together.

Video Time 5 minutes

[Show the Unit 1 video: "Our Journey"]

ASK: What stood out to you from the video?

[Allow the students to volunteer their answers.]

- N E X T -

Ideas to Try This Week

[Point out the ideas to try during the week.]

At home: Find some old family photos of your parents when they were your age. What emotions do you think your parents felt when they were younger? Show them your favorite photo and ask them about their life and faith when they were your age.

At school: Ask a friend to tell you about the last trip he or she took. Ask what he or she did to prepare for the journey and what the experience was like along the way. How does your friend's story relate to the confirmation journey you are beginning? What can you learn from your friend's experience?

In your community: Take a prayer walk around your neighborhood, remembering that God is with you every step of the way. Pause at least three times on your walk and say this prayer: "God, you are with me every step of the way. Continue to guide my faith as I enter my confirmation journey."

Confirm Teaching Plans

SURVIVAL CHART

Survival Elements	Use	How to Get It	Initial Here
Map (Schedule and Expectations)	This helps us know when we'll meet and what we'll focus on together.	Find 2 people wearing shoes similar to yours. **ASK:** Where is the farthest place you've traveled from home?	
A Pen	We'll draw and write to capture our thoughts and hopes along the journey.	Find 3 people you think have the most in common with you. **ASK:** What is your favorite activity outside of school? Why?	
Bible	Each time we gather, we'll look for wisdom and direction from the Scriptures.	Find 2 people with glasses or contact lenses. **ASK:** What do you hope to learn from confirmation?	
Guide Book (Student Guide)	We'll capture our experiences in this interactive journal.	Have EVERYONE in the room write his or her first and last name (clearly) on the back of this page.	No initials are needed. Write on the back of this page.
Snack	Throughout our journey, we'll enjoy tasty food that will help sustain us.	Find 3 people with the same hair or eye color as yours. **ASK:** What is your favorite sweet food? What is your favorite salty food?	
Travel Guide (Teacher)	We'll be surrounded by caring adults—teachers and mentors—who will help us along the journey.	Find EVERY ADULT in the room. **YOUR TURN TO ANSWER:** Why, do you think, is confirmation important? (Tell the adults.)	
Co-Travelers	We'll make new friends who will support us each step of the way.	Find 3 people you have never met or you know the least. **ASK:** What do you value most in a friend?	

Lesson

2 Living Together

LESSON DESCRIPTION: This lesson will continue to acclimate the teens with one another and others in the congregation. The introduction and explanation of the United Methodist membership vows will lay the foundation for teens accepting the responsibility of becoming active participants of the congregation. The teens will also be challenged to begin practicing what it means to uphold the membership vows and live in Christian community.

Lesson Outline

SECTION	TOPIC	DURATION
Connect	Hear and See	15 minutes
Explore	Defining Characteristics	12 minutes
Reflect	Living Together	10 minutes
Create	Confirmation, Community, and Covenant	25 minutes
Next	At home, at school, and in your community	Ideas to try this week

Supply List

Connect: Hear and See
- ❑ 3–5 congregation members, each with picture or special object
- ❑ Flip chart or a dry-erase board

Explore: Defining Characteristics
- ❑ Scripture reference note cards
- ❑ Bibles or Bible app
- ❑ Writing utensils
- ❑ A sign that says "Covenant" and a sign that says "Community"

Reflect: Living Together
- ❑ Student Guides
- ❑ Writing utensils

Create: Confirmation, Community, and Covenant
- ❑ 5 sheets of 8.5-by-11 paper or cardstock
- ❑ Standard-size sticky notes (about 20 notes per group of 3)
- ❑ Writing utensils

Next
- ❑ Student Guides

- C O N N E C T -

Hear and See *15 minutes*

[**LEADER PREP:** Ask 3–5 members of your congregation, from a variety of ages and stages in life, to do the following:

1. Share with a small group of teens a specific time when the church helped you connect with God through "prayers, presence, gifts, service, or witness."

2. Bring a photograph of that specific time (like a mission trip or baptism) or an object that represents that moment to them.

3. Be aware that the teens will be listening for the following:

   • The role God played in your experience.
   • The role the people of the church played in your experience.
   • Who or what was transformed through your experience.

Write the above three directives on a board so that they can be seen throughout the room.]

SAY: Today you are going to learn more about the people in our congregation. Let's have each of the people sharing introduce themselves, and tell us how long they have been members of the congregation.

[After each guest has introduced himself or herself, continue.]

SAY: Each of these congregation members is going to move to a different location around the room. You will have 3 minutes to talk with one of them about a specific time when the church helped them connect with God through "prayers, presence, gifts, service, or witness." They have brought with them a picture or special object that represents their experience. Use those items to help you determine whose story you would like to hear.

As you listen to their stories pay close attention to the following:

1. The role God played in the experience.

2. The role the people of the church played in the experience.

3. Who or what was transformed through the experience.

SAY: After you have heard the story, you will have another 3 minutes to talk with those classmates listening with you. Using what all of you heard, as a group you will be asked to retell the story of the congregation member focusing on God's role and the church's role in transformation.

[Once each group of teens has shared, invite the congregation members to offer any positive responses they had to the teens' retelling. Encourage teens and congregation members to continue the conversation after class.]

- E X P L O R E -

Defining Characteristics

12 minutes

[**LEADER PREP:** Write each of the following Scripture references on a note card.]

Community	**Covenant**
Hebrews 10:24-25	Genesis 9:12-17
Galatians 3:28-29	Leviticus 26:3-4, 11-13
Acts 2:46-47	Jeremiah 31:31-34
Colossians 3:12-17	Luke 22:14-20
Romans 15:5-7	Matthew 3:13-17
Ecclesiastes 4:9-12	Romans 8:37-39

[Give one note card to each teen in your group. If you have more teens than note cards, then assign each teen a partner. If you have fewer teens than note cards, give each teen more than one note card. On the right side of the room, place a sign on the wall with the word *Community* written on it. Do the same on the left side of the room with a sign with the word *Covenant*.]

SAY: You have been given a note card with a Scripture reference. Using a Bible or your Bible app, read the Scripture to yourself or with your partner. After reading decide whether the Scripture is talking about community or covenant. If you think that it's talking about community, move to the right side of the room. If you think it's talking about covenant, move to the left side of the room. For those not familiar with the word *covenant,* covenants are usually associated with promises or ways of being in relationship with God.

[Allow 2 minutes for the teens to read and move.]

SAY: Read your Scripture passage to the people on your side of the room. If your group thinks your passage is talking about the other topic, wait until all the Scripture passages are read before you move to the other side of the room. Based on all the passages read in your group, come up with a summary of what the Bible says about either community or covenant. Be prepared to share your summary with everyone.

[Allow the groups 8 minutes to read, summarize, and share.]

SAY: Thank you for taking time to think about these two important ideas that run through our Scripture. Covenant and community are two defining characteristics of living together with God and in the Church. The role of the community of Christians is to help one another stay faithful to the covenants we make with God. Without the shared covenants and support of our community, it would be nearly impossible to keep our promises with God.

This is a kind of covenant that we make with God and our brothers and sisters in Christ.

- R E F L E C T -

Living Together 10 minutes

SAY: If you decide to be confirmed in this church, then our membership vows are the things that you are going to promise to do and ways you are going to promise to live. It's important to know these from the start, so we're going to spend some time looking specifically at how we in the United Methodist community live together. You will find these membership vows in your Student Guide, and I'm going to ask you to turn to them now.

[Pick a teen to read the first membership vow and go around the room, having each teen read a vow until all of them have been read.]

SAY: Take a few minutes to look over these vows. Circle the words and phrases you are drawn to. Underline words and phrases you don't understand.

The following is from the Student Guide:

• To renounce the spiritual forces of wickedness, reject the evil powers of the world, and repent of their sin;

• To accept the freedom and power God gives them to resist evil, injustice, and oppression;

- To confess Jesus Christ as Savior, put their whole trust in his grace, and promise to serve him as their Lord;

- To remain faithful members of Christ's holy church and serve as Christ's representatives in the world;

- To be loyal to Christ through The United Methodist Church and do all in their power to strengthen its ministries;

- To faithfully participate in its ministries by their prayers, their presence, their gifts, their service, and their witness;

- To receive and profess the Christian faith as contained in the Scriptures of the Old and New Testaments.

- CREATE -

Confirmation, Community, and Covenant
25 minutes

> [**LEADER PREP:** Create a sign (8.5-by-11) for each of the five areas: prayers, presence, gifts, service, witness. Post them on the wall spaced out so students can place sticky notes around them.]

SAY: Right now we are going to focus on the vow to participate in our local church through prayers, presence, gifts, service, and witness. We will brainstorm ways to live out this vow during our confirmation journey. Our combined ideas will form a covenant that we will all commit to try our best to bring into reality.

Let's get into groups of 3 or 4 for this brainstorm.

> [Have students count off 1, 2, 3 to form their groups. Then give each group a stack of 20 or more sticky notes.]

SAY: You will be coming up with ideas in response to the five areas from this vow, listed in your student guide in the Create section: prayers, presence, gifts, service, and witness. Here are some instructions:

1. For each area, you will either write a word or draw a symbol (a small picture).

2. Each idea or symbol needs to be on a separate sticky note. For example, if you come up with "teacher" and "parents" as people we

Confirm Teaching Plans

need to prayer for, write those on separate sticky notes.

3. Work together with your groups to come up with as many ideas as you can in one minute.

Here is the first area:

1. **Prayers**—Contributing to your local church through prayer means that you will try to pray every day; for yourself, your church, and the people in your church.

SAY: Write down whom and what our group will pray for during this journey.

[Allow one minute for the students to complete the assignment.]

SAY: Post your ideas on the wall.

[Allow the students to post their notes.]

SAY: Now write down ways we could be fully present in our local church.

2. **Presence**—Participating in our local church through presence means that you show up fully in worship, Sunday school, and service and support of others in their journey with God. It is not just being the room, but it is engaging and seeking to connect with God and others.

[Allow one minute for the students to complete the assignment.]

SAY: Post your ideas on the wall.

[Allow the students to post their notes.]

SAY: Now write down ways we can financially support the work of the church here and all over the world.

3. **Gifts**—Participating in our local church through financial giving, even if it is just a small amount, signifies that all that you own and all that you are belongs to God. What if you were to give 10 percent of what you make? This practice, called tithing, seems like a little but symbolizes a lot.

[Allow one minute for the students to complete the assignment.]

SAY: Post your ideas on the wall.

[Allow the students to post their notes.]

SAY: Draw symbols or small sketches of ways we could serve the church during our confirmation journey. Provide a word or phrase description under each symbol.

4. Service—Participating in our local church through service means discovering your spiritual gifts and using those spiritual gifts in the church and with the church.

[Allow one minute for the students to complete the assignment.]

SAY: Post your ideas on the wall.

[Allow the students to post their notes.]

SAY: Now write down ways we could show and tell others about our faith.

5. Witness—Participating in our local church through witness is simply inviting other people to experience God's love (maybe not exclusively in your church) and walking with them as they become disciples of Jesus Christ. Another way to think about what it means to be a witness is to say we are ambassadors for Christ, to live so others see Christ through us.

[Allow one minute for the students to complete the assignment.]

SAY: Post your ideas on the wall.

[Allow the students to post their notes.]

SAY: Great job! You came up with so many good ideas. Now let's work together to pick our favorite ideas. This might be hard, because all of them are strong. Our favorite ideas will be a part of our covenant—they will be things we commit together to try and live out.

Come up to the sticky notes and put a star on your favorite idea for each of the 5 areas.

[After students "star" their favorites, tally the favorites and determine the top three ideas for each area.]

SAY: OK, here are the top 3 ideas for each area of this vow. Write these areas in your Student Guide.

[Read the top 3 ideas for prayers, presence, gifts, service, and witness.]

[After class, ask an artistic teen to create one poster listing the five areas and the two or three ways the group has

Confirm Teaching Plans

committed to that area. Keep this poster visible for the duration of confirmation.]

SAY: Let's commit together to covenant to make these ideas a reality in this community and help each other stay accountable to them. We may not all be able to keep these commitments 100 percent of the time, but we are going to promise one another and God that we will do our best for the benefit of this community.

Let's pray together:

Dear God,

We confess that we have a lot going on in our lives and taking on one more commitment doesn't seem possible. But we want to do this for you and for each other. Bless these promises we have made, help us to keep them, and be graceful and understanding when one of us breaks our promise. Let this covenant remind us of your unending love and commitment to us.

In Jesus' name we pray. Amen.

Discussion Question

• Which of these five areas are you most excited about? Why?

- N E X T -

Ideas to Try This Week

[Point out the ideas to try during the week.]

At home: Talk with your family about the norms and expectations you share. Whether it's official or unofficial, what is your family covenant? Lead your family through some of the questions you discussed in this confirmation lesson and create a family covenant together.

At school: Think about a time when you felt like you belonged at school, either your current school or another school you went to. What about that time made you feel connected? Who helped you to feel like you were part of something more than yourself? What could you do to help others feel a sense of belonging at school this week?

In your community: Introduce yourself to your neighbors. Whether you know them or not, knock on their door and say hello. Ask them what it means for them to be a part of the community. And then tell them what it means for you! (Hint: If your family does not know the people who live around you, be sure to talk to your parents or guardians before you knock on a strangers' door. You might want to bring an adult along.)

Confirm Teaching Plans

Lesson

3   Loving Together

LESSON DESCRIPTION: This lesson will build on the concept of living together in the midst of differences from the previous lesson, Living Together. This lesson will push teens to consider how coming together in Christian love can be a strong witness to God's love for all.

Lesson Outline		
SECTION	**TOPIC**	**DURATION**
Connect	#Christian	15 minutes
Explore	The New Commandment	20 minutes
	Lesson 3 video: "Loving Together"	5 minutes
Reflect	Showing Love	10 minutes
Create	"Show Love to Others" Day	15 minutes
Next	At home, at school, and in your community	Ideas to try this week

Supply List

Connect: #Christian
❑ Access to social media

Explore: The New Commandment:
❑ Bibles (print or digital)
❑ Copies of "The New Commandment" handout
❑ Lesson 3 video: "Loving Together"

Reflect: Showing Love
❑ Student Guides
❑ Drawing utensils

Create: 'Show Love to Others' Day
❑ Student Guides
❑ Writing utensils

Next
❑ Student Guides

- C O N N E C T -

#Christian *15 minutes*

SAY: Sometimes you may wonder, what exactly does a Christian look like? Should you be able to tell if someone is Christian just by looking? Should you be able to tell what a Christian believes by looking through his or her social media posts? Today we're going to explore what a Christian is and how our interactions with the world can be a reflection to God's love.

We are going to start with an online image search. You will need to select one social media platform (Snapchat, Instagram, Twitter, and so on) and search for pictures depicting Christians. You may do this individually or with a partner if you don't have a way to connect with social media today. You or your group have 5 minutes to find the best single visual representation of what a Christian looks like. You will be asked to show your picture to everyone and explain why you selected it.

   [Allow a few minutes for the students to search for and select images, the ask students to do the following:]

• Show the visual representations, and explain why they selected them.

• Highlight anything that seems particularly interesting or concerning.

• Tell how they think digital communities are shaping the public perception of Christians.

SAY: Oftentimes, we are quick to categorize or define people by how they look, what they say, and even how they act. If this is the world that we live in, where our appearance, words, and actions are used to classify and define us, then how can we tell whether someone is a follower of Christ? How are we showing others that we are followers of Christ?

- E X P L O R E -

The New Commandment *20 minutes*

SAY: For thousands of years before Jesus, the people of God lived by a set of rules—called commands and laws—that set them apart from the rest of the world. You would know that someone was a follower of God if the person lived by these commands. But people often lost focus of what these commands really meant.

So when Jesus came, he refocused everyone on God's way of life and summed up all of the laws and commands in a "New Commandment." Let's take a look at what Jesus said.

I need two volunteers to read Scripture aloud. The first volunteer will read John 13:34-35 and the second volunteer will read John 15:9-17.

[Divide the teens into two groups: a "commandment" group and a "love" group. Hand out the "New Commandment" handout.]

SAY: Listen carefully as these Scriptures are read. Each time you hear the word *command* or *commandments,* the command group must stand and the love group must sit. Each time you hear the word *love* or *loved,* the command group must sit and the love group must stand. If either word is repeated while the corresponding group remains standing, that group must hop up and down until the other word is said.

[After reading the Scripture aloud with the teens doing the actions, ask each group to read the Scripture aloud again within their group, without doing the actions. Then have the group answer the following questions together and prepare to share their answers with the other group.]

• How does "love each other just as I have loved you" provide an outline for how Christians live?

• How do "love" and "commands" balance each other out? How do they make living for God more manageable?

• Using the images those in your group selected in the opening activity, work together to tell a story of how all these people found each other and worked together to share God's love.

• What are some ways we could be "known by our love for each other"?

SAY: Thanks for working together on that. It's most often easy for us to love those who love us, even when they annoy us. It's more difficult to love people we don't know or don't like. However, this is the kind of love Jesus had for others and what he calls his followers to exhibit. Now we're going to watch a short video that may give us some more information about what it looks like to love like Jesus loves.

Video Time 5 minutes

[Show the Lesson 3 video: "Loving Together."]

ASK: What stood out to you from the video?

- R E F L E C T -

Showing Love *10 minutes*

SAY: Complete the lists in the Reflect section of your Student Guide.

- C R E A T E -

'Show Love to Others' Day *15 minutes*

SAY: Pair up to do the Create section in your Student Guide.

[Allow the pairs about 12 minutes to do the activity in pairs.]

Discussion Questions *As Time Allows*

• What was your favorite part that you developed with your partner?

• How, do you think, would your family and friends respond to a day like the one you described?

• What makes it difficult to have days like this one all the time?

• What does a day like this have to do with being a Christian?

- N E X T -

Ideas to Try This Week

[Point out the ideas to try during the week.]

At home: Think of one thing you can do to show love to everyone in your immediate family. Do at least one of those things each day this week.

At school: Revisit one scene from the love-filled day you created. Be intentional about bringing this scene to life. Afterwards take some time to journal about this experience. Did the scene play out like you expected? What surprised you? What would you do differently next time?

In your community: One way to love your community is to make it a lovely place to live. Walk around your neighborhood and do something to make your neighbor's life less stressful. Take 20 minutes to pick up trash, rake leaves, remove snow, spread mulch, sweep steps or sidewalks. What impact does a lovely environment have on the whole community? How will your neighbor be affected by your help?

THE NEW COMMANDMENT

JOHN 13:34-35: [34] "I give you a new commandment: Love each other. Just as I have loved you, so you also must love each other. [35] This is how everyone will know that you are my disciples, when you love each other."

JOHN 15:9-17: [9] "As the Father loved me, I too have loved you. Remain in my love. [10] If you keep my commandments, you will remain in my love, just as I kept my Father's commandments and remain in his love. [11] I have said these things to you so that my joy will be in you and your joy will be complete. [12] This is my commandment: love each other just as I have loved you. [13] No one has greater love than to give up one's life for one's friends. [14] You are my friends if you do what I command you. [15] I don't call you servants any longer, because servants don't know what their master is doing. Instead, I call you friends, because everything I heard from my Father I have made known to you. [16] You didn't choose me, but I chose you and appointed you so that you could go and produce fruit and so that your fruit could last. As a result, whatever you ask the Father in my name, he will give you. [17] I give you these commandments so that you can love each other."

- How does "love each other just as I have loved you" provide an outline for how Christians live?

- How do "love" and "commands" balance each other out? How do they make living for God more manageable?

- Using the images those in your group selected in the opening activity, work together to tell a story of how all these people found each other and worked together to share God's love?

- What are some ways we could be "known by our love for each other"?

Lesson

4 Belonging Together

LESSON DESCRIPTION: This final lesson of the opening unit will tie together being part of a community of Christians with belonging to God. Teens will evaluate their interest in being part of a faith community as well as being in a relationship with God. They will also explore how their connection with God and the community are both necessary for being able to continue their faith journey.

Lesson Outline		
SECTION	*TOPIC*	*DURATION*
Connect	Where Are You Now?	15 minutes
	Lesson 4 video: "Belonging Together"	5 minutes
Explore	You Belong to Me	20 minutes
Reflect	Different Journeys	5 minutes
Create	My Faith Map	15 minutes
Next	At home, at school, and in your community	Ideas to try this week

Supply List

Connect: Where Are You Now?
❑ Copies of the "Where Are You Now?" evaluation survey
❑ Writing utensils
❑ Lesson 4 video: "Belonging Together"

Explore: You Belong to Me
❑ A copy of the "Belonging Scripture Cards" (cut apart)
❑ Tape

Reflect: Different Journeys
❑ Student Guides
❑ Writing utensils

Create: My Faith Map
❑ Student Guides
❑ Writing utensils
❑ Markers or colored pencils

Next
❑ Student Guides

- C O N N E C T -

Where Are You Now? *15 minutes*

[Hand a copy of the evaluation page to each participant.]

SAY: As we begin our time together today, you are going to fill out a 5-question evaluation. You will in no way be asked or required to share your answers to these questions. In an effort to practice living together in Christian trust and loyalty, please respect the privacy of one another.

[Allow time for the students to fill out the evaluation.]

SAY: As you know, there's more to being a Christian than belonging to a church. The most profound part of being a Christian is that you belong to God. It's not something that you earn; you are a child of God by the very fact that God created you and loves you. We are going to watch a video about belonging to God.

[Collect the evaluations and store them in a safe place so that they can be viewed in the final lesson, Lesson 39.]

Video Time *5 minutes*

[Show the Lesson 4 video: "Belonging Together."]

Discussion Questions

[After viewing the video, discuss the following questions.]

• What did you connect with from the video? How did the video make you feel?

• How might knowing that we belong to God change how we see ourselves? How might it help us when we are going through difficult times?

SAY: As we have learned, part of the responsibility of being in a community of believers is practicing Christ-like love toward one another. We have the power to live like this because we were created in the image of a loving and grace-filled God. We just saw several of the Scripture passages that talk about our belonging to God. Let's look more closely at a few to see if we can get a better understanding of what it means to be a child of God.

- E X P L O R E -

You Belong to Me 20 minutes

[**LEADER PREP:** Copy the "Belonging Scripture Cards" and cut apart the cards on the dotted lines so that you have 10 halves of Scripture passages,.

The following Scriptures are on the Belonging Scripture Cards: Isaiah 43:1-4; Isaiah 43:10-13; Jeremiah 29:11-14; John 15:1-8; 1 John 5:1-5.

Mix up the pieces.]

SAY: I need five volunteers to read some Scripture passages aloud.

[Have each student volunteer pick up two random cards of the Belonging Scripture Cards and read them one after another or put the two cards side-by-side and read across both of them. Repeat until all of the cards have been read.]

Discussion Questions

• What sense can you make of these disconnected pieces of Scripture?

• What can you determine about God from these bits and pieces of Scripture?

[Challenge the group to reassemble the pieces into the 5 complete passages. When they have done so, have them tape the pairs of cards together. Then ask five volunteers to read each aloud in its entirety.]

[After each card is read, ask the following questions.]

• What does this tell us about God's feelings toward us as children of God?

• What does this tell us about committing to a relationship with God?

SAY: Just like when the Scriptures were apart and we couldn't make sense of what was going on, if we separate ourselves from God and from the community of faith, our actions lose their sense of purpose and we lose our focus on Who we are serving.

- R E F L E C T -

Different Journeys 5 minutes

SAY: Since we are each on a different journey with God, we will connect with different parts of Scripture. Of the five passages we just read, select the one passage that made the most sense to you. Using the space provided in your Student Guide, draw a picture or create a word cloud of the image that came into your mind when you heard the Scripture.

ASK: Why did you choose this passage? What does it say to you about belonging?

- C R E A T E -

My Faith Map 15 minutes

[Ask a volunteer to read the following instructions for this activity from the Student Guide.]

The following instructions are from the Student Guide:

Draw a map that follows your spiritual formation journey. Be sure to include your current location ("You are here!") and all the twists and turns (and dead ends) that it entails. What are the potholes, speed bumps, wrong turns, and one-way streets in your faith journey? And who has been with you along the way?

Discussion Questions

As Time Allows

- If you had to pick one thing from your map that has impacted you most, what would it be?

- Looking at your completed map, what surprised you about your faith journey?

- Where do you think your faith journey will take you in the future? How do you feel about the future?

- N E X T -

Ideas to Try This Week

[Point out the ideas to try during the week.]

At home: Share your Faith Map with your family. Point out the specific ways that your family has been influential on your faith journey. Then lead your family in creating a Family Faith Map. How does your family's faith journey compare with your own?

At school: Practice belonging this week by inviting two or three people to hang out with you and your friends. Invite people you don't typically spend time with and people you think would appreciate making some new friends. Why is "belonging together" important for someone's faith journey?

In your community: Find out what belonging means to someone in your church community. Spend some time talking with a member of your congregation about why belonging to your congregation is important to him or her and how it has made a difference in his or her life.

Confirm Teaching Plans

WHERE ARE YOU NOW?

Circle the answer that best fits your response. You will in no way be asked or required to share your answers to these questions. In an effort to practice living together in Christian trust and loyalty, please respect the privacy of one another.

1. **On a scale of 1–5, how important do you think this confirmation journey is to your life?**

1–unimportant

2–somewhat unimportant

3–neither unimportant nor important

4–important

5–very important

2. **On a scale of 1–5, how comfortable do you feel with the people in your church?**

1–uncomfortable

2–somewhat uncomfortable

3–neither uncomfortable nor comfortable

4–comfortable

5–very comfortable

3. **On a scale of 1–5, how supported do you feel by the adults in your church?**

1–unsupported

2–somewhat unsupported

3–neither unsupported nor supported

4–supported

5–very supported

4. **On a scale of 1–5, how much do you want to belong to a faith community?**

1–not at all

2–not important

3–no opinion

4–guess it would be fine

5–very much want to belong

5. **On a scale of 1–5, how close do you feel to God?**

1–very distant

2–somewhat distant

3–neither distant nor close

4–somewhat close

5–very close

BELONGING
SCRIPTURE CARDS

Isaiah 43:1-4

But now,	says the LORD—
the one who	created you, Jacob,
the one who	formed you, Israel:
Don't fear, for	I have redeemed you;
I have called you	by name; you are mine.
When you pass through	the waters, I will be with you;
when through the rivers,	they won't sweep over you.
When you walk through the fire,	you won't be scorched
and flame won't	burn you.
I am the LORD	your God,
the holy one of	Israel, your savior.
I have given Egypt	as your ransom,
Cush and Seba	in your place.
Because you are	precious in my eyes,
you are honored,	and I love you.
I give people	in your place,
and nations in	exchange for your life.

Isaiah 43:10-13

You are my	witnesses, says the LORD,
my servant,	whom I chose,
so that you would	know and believe me
and understand	that I am the one.
Before me no	god was formed;
after me there	has been no other.
I, I am	the LORD,
and there is no	savior besides me.
I announced, I	saved, I proclaimed,
not some stranger	among you.
You are my witnesses,	says the LORD,
and I	am God.
From the dawn of	time, I am the one.
No one can	escape my power.
I act, and	who can undo it?

Jeremiah 29:11-14

I know the plans | I have in mind
for you, declares | the LORD; they
are plans for | peace, not disaster,
to give you a | future filled with
hope. When you | call me and
come and pray | to me, I will
listen to you. | When you search
for me, yes, | search for me with
all your heart, | you will find
me. I will be | present for you,
declares the LORD, | and I will
end your captivity. | I will gather
you from all | the nations and
places where | I have scattered
you, and I will bring | you home after
your long exile, | declares the LORD.

John 15:1-8

I am the true vine, and my | Father is the vineyard keeper.
He removes any of my branches | that don't produce fruit,
and he trims any branch | that produces fruit so that it
will produce even more | fruit. You are already trimmed
because of the word I have | spoken to you. Remain in me,
and I will remain in you. | A branch can't produce fruit by
itself, but must remain in | the vine. Likewise, you can't
produce fruit unless you | remain in me. I am the vine;
you are the branches. | If you remain in me and I in you,
then you will produce much | fruit. Without me, you can't
do anything. If you don't | remain in me, you will be like a
branch that is thrown out | and dries up. Those branches
are gathered up, thrown into | a fire, and burned. If you
remain in me and my words | remain in you, ask for
whatever you want and it | will be done for you. My Father
is glorified when you produce | much fruit and in this way
prove that you | are my disciples.

1 John 5:1-5

Everyone who believes | that Jesus is
the Christ has been | born from God.
Whoever loves someone | who is a parent
loves the child | born to the
parent. This is how | we know that we
love the children of | God: when we love
God and keep | God's commandments.
This is the love of | God: we keep God's
commandments. | God's commandments
are not difficult, | because everyone who
is born from God | defeats the world.
And this is the victory | that has defeated
the world: our faith. | Who defeats the
world? Isn't it the one | who believes that
Jesus is | God's Son?

Unit 2: Our History and Heritage

In order to truly understand our lives and beliefs we must understand the lives and beliefs of the people who came before us. Our identity and faith is rooted in and shaped by the experiences of our spiritual ancestors traced back over the centuries.

These six lessons are designed to help you consider where your faith comes from in the hope that it will give you a better understanding of where it may be going. You'll be introduced to a long and diverse tradition that you're already a part of, and encouraged to imagine how you might carry that tradition into the future.

- C O N T E N T S -

Lesson

5 The Faith of Jesus

LESSON DESCRIPTION: This lesson will introduce the students to Unit 2: Our History and Heritage as well as exploring the (Jewish) faith of Jesus. The lesson will be framed with the story of Jesus' own time spent in the temple learning from his elders as a young boy. It will explore the history of the Israelites and will prepare students for their own journey into the history of Christian and specifically Methodist faith.

Lesson Outline

SECTION	TOPIC	DURATION
Connect	2,000 Years Is a Long Time	15 minutes
	Unit 2 video: "Our History and Heritage"	5 minutes
Explore	The Story of Israel	20 minutes
Reflect	Reading as Prayer	10 minutes
Create	Show and Tell	15 minutes
Next	At home, at school, and in your community	Ideas to try this week

Supply List

Connect: 2,000 Years Is a Long Time
❑ 2 pieces of sheets of flip chart paper. Label them "The Faith of Jesus" and " Our Faith Now"
❑ Markers
❑ Unit 2 video: "Our History and Heritage"

Explore: The Story of Israel
❑ Bibles

Reflect: Reading as Prayer
❑ Bible
❑ Student Guides
❑ Writing utensils

Create: Show and Tell
❑ Student Guides
❑ Drawing utensils

Next
❑ Student Guides

- C O N N E C T -

Video Time 5 minutes

[Show the Unit 2 video: "Our History and Heritage."]

ASK: What stood out to you from the video?

2,000 Years Is a Long Time 15 minutes

[**LEADER PREP:** Post 2 sheets of flip chart paper side by side on the wall before the students enter (a dry-erase board or chalkboard could also be used). Write "The Faith of Jesus" at the top of the paper on the left and "Our Faith Now" on the top of the paper on the right.]

SAY: How many of you have stared at a clock waiting for a class to end? Did it feel like time had slowed to a crawl? Maybe even stopped and gone in reverse? That's one of the problems with time; it never speeds up when you need it to. In fact, it never speeds up at all. There's no fast-forward button on life; and that tricks us into thinking that every moment is the most important, every crisis is the worst and every event is the biggest ever.

It's hard to have perspective, to look at the long, slow march of time and see how each moment, each crisis, and each event builds on top of the last one to bring us here. That's what the next six lessons are about. We're going to talk about the history of the church, the history of faith, and how we're part of the history of those who are yet to be born. To get us started, let's watch a quick video introducing the next few lessons.

[You will be asking students some questions about the Jewish faith at the time of Jesus. Give the students a minute to name answers aloud. Remind the students that it's OK if they don't know a lot already. It's expected that they won't know much. If they don't have any answers, prompt them with the answers that follow each question. Assign someone to summarize them on the sheet of flip chart paper labeled "The Faith of Jesus."]

SAY: We're going to start our look at the history of faith by talking about the faith of Jesus. Jesus was born into the Jewish faith, which you may be familiar with because it's the faith of Abraham, Isaac, Jacob, and most of the other people you've heard about in Sunday school. Let's look at what you know about the Jewish faith at the time of Jesus. Who'd be willing to summarize our answers on the board under the "The Faith of Jesus" section?

• Do you know where Jewish people at the Jesus' time worshipped?

Most communities would meet in synagogues, which were local buildings set aside for religious ceremonies and instruction. Synagogues would often serve as schools as well.

[Ask a volunteer to write the word *synagogue* on the board.]

However, on special feast days, especially Passover and the Day of Atonement, many Jewish people would travel to the Temple in Jerusalem to participate in the religious festivals and ceremonies. We'll talk more about the Temple in the next activity. (Ask the student volunteer to write "Temple in Jerusalem" on the board.)

• What important holidays or celebrations did they have?

The Jewish people had several holy days set aside to remember God's acts throughout their history. There were seven festivals including Passover, the Festival of Unleavened Bread, the Feast of First Fruits, the Feast of Weeks, the Feast of Trumpets, the Day of Atonement, and the Festival of Booths. The most important of these was Passover, when the people would remember God leading them out of Egypt. You can learn more about these festivals in Leviticus 23.

• What did they study to learn about God?

They would have studied the books that make up what we call the Old Testament. It was typically divided into three parts: the Law (Torah), the Prophets (Nevi'im), and the Writings (Kethuvium). Memorization and dialogue were very important in studying the Scriptures for Jewish leaders. But the vast majority of Jewish people were unable to read or write, so they learned about God mostly through stories passed down from family, and teaching from the rabbis in the synagogue. Each week, rabbis and Jewish leaders read Scriptures, told stories about the faith, and gave commentaries (called Midrash) about the Scriptures.

SAY: We should remember that Jesus was born more than 2,000 years ago. While we have the Bible to tell us a lot about that time, as well as history books and archaeologists, there is still a lot that's not been documented. Let's think about Our Faith Now. I need someone to summarize our answers on the board. These questions may seem obvious, but let's brainstorm as many answers as we can.

- How would you describe where we worship? How do we worship?

- What important traditions and holidays do we celebrate as Christians?

- What traditions (and practices) do we have as Methodists?

- How do we study the Bible? How do we learn about God?

Discussion Questions

- What seems similar between the faith of Jesus and our faith? What is different?

- What do you think people 2,000 years from now will think about the place and way we worship?

- What do you think they'll see as strange that we see as being normal?

- How does this help you gain perspective on your own faith?

- EXPLORE -
The Story of Israel *20 minutes*

SAY: You might find confirmation strange. Maybe you're the only one of your friends at school who's going through it. But there's a long legacy of people who at your age committed to a special group to learn more about their faith, ask questions, and look for answers. Even Jesus went through something similar in the book of Luke. Who would be willing to read Luke 2:41-52 aloud for us?

[Have a volunteer student read Luke 2:41-52 aloud.]

SAY: To get a sense of what Jesus would have been learning in the temple, we will be reading aloud from several important passages in the Old Testament which help to tell the story of God's people. I will need five volunteers to read the Scripture aloud.

[Have the volunteers find and mark their passages before you read the next section. The first volunteer will read Nehemiah 9:1-13. The second, Nehemiah 9:14-25. The third, Micah 6:1-8. The fourth, Nehemiah 9:26-38. The fifth will read Isaiah 9:1-7.]

SAY: Before we read these passages it might help to know a little about the world where Jesus grew up. Centuries before Jesus was born, King Nebuchadnezzar of Babylon conquered Israel, exiled the people, and destroyed the temple. After 150 years, a man named Nehemiah was allowed to bring some of the people back to repair the walls of Jerusalem and to rebuild the temple. However, the people of Israel were never truly free of their captors. The rule of Babylon gave way to the rule of the Persians and then the Greeks, and eventually, decades before Jesus' birth, the Romans came to power. By the time Jesus heard these words his people, the Israelites, had been dispersed all over the empire, and the nation of Israel had been under the thumb of a ruling nation for 600 years.

SAY: When Nehemiah and his small group of Israelites returned to Jerusalem, they rededicated themselves to their faith and their tradition. Our first two readings are from the Book of Nehemiah, where the people collectively remember their history and repent of their sins. As you listen to these Scriptures, imagine that you are in the Temple with Jesus, possibly hearing these words for the first time. Jesus is sitting in the same temple that Nehemiah built after returning from exile more than 400 years ago and learning the same story of faith that his people had passed down for generations. Think about what these words would have meant to someone in his situation.

[Have the first two volunteers read Nehemiah 9:1-13 and Nehemiah 9:14-25 aloud.]

SAY: Despite God's goodness, the Israelites still wanted things their own way; and so God sent prophets to bring them back to God. This next reading is from one of those prophets, a man named Micah.

[Have the third volunteer read Micah 6:1-8 aloud.]

SAY: But the people did not listen to Micah's words; they did not do justice, embrace faithful love, or walk humbly with their God. Let's pick up the story again in Nehemiah.

[Have the fourth volunteer read Nehemiah 9:26-38 aloud.]

SAY: This was still the situation in the time of Jesus. The Babylonians no longer ruled Israel, but the Romans had taken over and Israel remained an occupied nation. Yet there was still a promise for the future and a hope.

[Have the fifth volunteer read Isaiah 9:1-7 aloud.]

Discussion Questions

- What stuck out to you from the story of Israel?

- What did you find important?

- How did some of the passages make you feel?

- What, do you think, would these words have meant to Jesus?

- R E F L E C T -
Reading as Prayer 10 minutes

SAY: We're going to try something that you may never have done before. It's called *lectio divina* (LEK-tsea-oh di-VEEN-ah), which is Latin for "divine reading." It's a way to meditate on a particular passage of Scripture.

The passage we're going to focus on was a very important part of Jesus' Jewish faith. It's a prayer called the Shema (shem-AH) that's found in the book of Deuteronomy. I'm going to read through this prayer three times and you'll focus on something different each time. For the first time, just listen to the Scripture and let it wash over you.

   [Read Deuteronomy 6:4-9 aloud at a steady pace.]

SAY: Take a deep breath, relax. This time I want you to pick out a word or phrase that jumps out to you.

   [Read Deuteronomy 6:4-9 aloud again at a steady pace.]

SAY: Take another deep breath, close your eyes, and focus on the word or phrase you picked while I read through one more time.

   [Read Deuteronomy 6:4-9 a final time, a bit slower than the first two times.]

SAY: In your student guides, write a few sentences about the word or phrase you picked and what you noticed about these verses. Think about how this prayer connects to the history of Israel we talked about earlier.

   [Give the students 3–5 minutes to write. Then invite a few of them to share if they would like to.]

- C R E A T E -
Show and Tell 15 minutes

ASK: Who'd be willing to read the instructions aloud for the Create activity in your Student Guide?

[Let the volunteer read. Then allow time for students to ask any questions they may have about the assignment.]

SAY: Take about 10 minutes to complete this activity. Go!

[Allow time for students to work on their own.]

SAY: Let's come back together and share our creations.

Discussion Questions As Time Allows

• Who'd be willing to share what you created?

• What did you like about this activity? What was challenging?

• What did you learn today that will stay with you?

- N E X T -

Ideas to Try This Week

[Point out the ideas to try during the week.]

At home: Lead your family in the Reflect and Create activities. Invite them to read Deuteronomy 6:4-9 and capture a word or phrase. Then invite them to create an image or illustration on one half of a blank piece of paper. Have them swap with another family member and draw their image or illustration again.

At school: Find your history teacher and ask how learning about the past affects our present and our future. What is the significance of remembering our heritage? How does this shape our future? Take notes on what this teacher says and share them at your next confirmation class.

In your community: Research the history and heritage of your community. Visit the library, search online, and talk with your neighbors about what they remember about the history and heritage of your community. What difference does it make to know the history of the place you call home?

Lesson

6 The Early Church

LESSON DESCRIPTION: This lesson will give the students an overview of church history from the beginning of the church to just before the Reformation. The lesson will both explore the broad scope of church history and allow the students to connect personally with some of the more important figures in Christian history. Finally, this lesson will try and connect the story of the church's formation and expansion to the faith of students today.

Lesson Outline

SECTION	TOPIC	DURATION
Connect	What's In a Name?	10 minutes
Explore	The Expansion of the Church	15 minutes
	Lesson 6 video: "The Early Church"	10 minutes
Reflect	Great Cloud of Witnesses	5 minutes
Create	Lights, Camera, Action!	15 minutes
Next	At home, at school, and in your community	Ideas to try this week

Supply List

Connect: What's in a Name?
- ❑ Roman pictures and decorations
- ❑ Sheet of flip chart paper
- ❑ Sticky notes
- ❑ Writing utensils

Explore: The Expansion of the Church
- ❑ A handful of small prizes (such as candy) for the "Name That Christian" game
- ❑ Internet-capable devices such as smartphones and tablets
- ❑ Lesson 6 video: "The Early Church"

Reflect: Great Cloud of Witnesses
- ❑ Student Guides
- ❑ Writing utensils

Create: Lights, Camera, Action!
- ❑ Student Guides
- ❑ Writing utensils
- ❑ Internet-capable devices such as smartphones and tablets

Next
- ❑ Student Guides

- C O N N E C T -

What's in a Name 10 minutes

[**LEADER PREP:** To set the mood for your lesson this week, consider decorating the room in a Roman style. This may be as simple as posting pictures of Roman emperors, statues, and architecture around the room, projecting a video or images showcasing Rome, or even a PowerPoint presentation of Roman images on a loop as students enter class.

Before class begins, prepare for the naming activity. You will need pens, enough sticky notes for each student to have one, and a sheet of flip chart paper posted on the wall titled, "What's in a Name?"]

SAY: Last week we talked about how, in the time of Jesus, Israel was under Roman occupation. Rome was the most powerful empire in the world. As the church expanded and grew it became increasingly intertwined with Rome. At first, this was very dangerous. One of the early leaders of the church, Paul, was arrested for preaching the gospel and eventually executed in Rome. About 200 years later, the Roman emperor Diocletian persecuted and killed many Christians.

But Christianity became stronger and stronger in the Roman Empire and became the official religion in A.D. 380. Christianity expanded wherever Rome went; and as a result, much of the church's history is tied to the history of the Roman Empire. This means that a lot of the earliest Christian writers and leaders wrote and spoke Latin and the earliest translations of the Bible were in Latin. People like Jerome are remembered for translating the Bible into Latin, while others like Augustine and Tertullian are remembered for their explanation of faith and theology.

In Roman times, sculpture and art played a central role in culture. Many of these sculptures would be dedicated to famous people in honor of the great things they had done in their lives. For instance, a sculpture might be dedicated to Tertullian, the father of Latin Christianity, or Jerome, the father of biblical translation.

[Hand out sticky notes. Explain the format for writing out the students' Latin names.]

SAY: To prepare for our lesson about the early church, everyone is going to find their own Latin name.

Lesson 6

- For the boys, take the first four letters of your middle name and add either "ius" or "ian."

- For the girls, take the first three letters of your middle name and add either "ia" or "illa."

Choose whichever option you think is most fun; and if you like them both, then use them both and have a double name. On the sticky notes I provided, write "To (your Latin name), mother/father of" and leave a blank. We'll get to that part in just a second. Write your name on the sticky note now.

[Give the students a minute to write down their Latin names.]

SAY: Now the name is only the first part. The next part is what you want to be remembered for. Take a couple of minutes and write on the back of the sticky note what you hope would be written on a statue of you 1,000 years in the future.

[Give the students 2 minutes to write down what they want to be remembered for. Have them post the sticky notes on the flip chart paper, and leave it on the wall throughout the rest the History and Heritage unit. Let a few students share their names. Prompt some of the shyer students to share if they feel comfortable.]

- E X P L O R E -

Video Time *10 minutes*

SAY: The story of the church is long and filled with many twists and turns. There are countless teachers and preachers, writers and monks, kings and queens who play a role in the history of the church. It's filled with tales of war and political intrigue, but also boundless love and beauty. People spend years and years trying to understand it and piece it together. Unfortunately, we don't have quite that much time, so we're going to give you the 180-second version of the rise of the church.

[Show the Lesson 6 video: "The Early Church."]

ASK: What stood out to you from the video?

SAY: That's a lot to information to take in, so let's discuss what we've learned.

Confirm Teaching Plans

Discussion Questions

• What was the most important thing that you learned from the video?

• What were you surprised to learn?

• What questions do you have after learning about this history?

• How, do you think, does this history apply to you and your faith?

The Expansion of the Church 15 minutes

SAY: In order to learn a little bit more about some of the important people from the history of the church, we're going to play a game called "Name That Christian." In each round, I'm going to give you clues about a particularly important person in church history. You'll have to search online to discover whom the clue applies to. Whoever gets the right answer first will win a prize. There are four clues for each person, and the clues get easier as we go, but that means it'll be easier for everyone else to find them too. Ready?

[Read the bulleted clues (below) one at a time, leaving 30–45 seconds after each clue to give the students time to search. If a student guesses the answer, give him or her a small prize, such as a piece of candy. If a student guesses before you give all of the clues, remember to tell the students the rest of the information about the person in question. The clues for each person are listed below his or her name.]

Augustine
• Early Christian theologian and philosopher
• Was a bishop of the church in Africa
• "The Bible was composed in such a way that as beginners mature, its meaning grows with them.
• Wrote the first Christian memoir, *Confessions*

Gregory the Great
• Gave away his family's abundant wealth and became a monk
• Is known as the father of Christian worship
• Sent Augustine of Canterbury on a mission to convert the Britains
• Became Pope of the Catholic Church in A.D. 590

Julian of Norwich
• Lived a monastic lifestyle
• Nearly died and had a mystical encounter with God

- The saying "All shall be well and all shall be well, and all manner of things shall be well" is attributed to her.
- Wrote *Revelations of Divine Love*

Francis of Assisi
- Is the patron saint of Italy
- Lived a monastic lifestyle and founded the Order of the Friars' Minor
- "Start by doing what is necessary, then what is possible, and suddenly you are doing the impossible."
- The current Pope of the Catholic Church is named after him (*This clue is from 2016. Please update this clue if Pope Francis is not the Pope.*)

- R E F L E C T -
Great Cloud of Witnesses *5 minutes*

SAY: Today we've learned about some of the people who have been part of the story of the church, and as a result, part of the story of our faith. Now I want you to imagine what it would be like to meet one of these people, to have dinner with him or her, and to ask anything you want about his or her life and faith.

Choose one person from the list in your Student Guide that you would like to have dinner with. Where or what would you eat? And what are three questions that you would ask this person?

SAY: Now turn to your Student Guide, and record your choices in the Reflect section.

- C R E A T E -
Lights, Camera, Action! *15 minutes*

SAY: Who'd be willing to read the instructions aloud for the Create activity in your Student Guide?

[Ask the volunteer to read the instructions aloud.]

SAY: Take about 10 minutes to complete this activity. Go!

[Allow about 10 minutes for the students to work on their own.]

SAY: Let's come back together and share our creations.

Discussion Questions *As Time Allows*

• Who would be willing to share what you created?

• What did you like about this activity? What was challenging?

• What did you learn today that will stay with you?

- N E X T -

Ideas to Try This Week

[Point out the ideas to try during the week.]

At home: Go online and research more about the person from church history you selected in the Reflect section. Write down notes from what you learn and share them at the next confirmation class.

At school: Summarize today's lesson in five words. Share them with five different people at school.

In your community: Find some sidewalk chalk and recreate the church history timeline on the sidewalk in your community. Invite your neighbors to join you as you literally walk through the history of the church.

Lesson

7 The Reformation

LESSON DESCRIPTION: In this lesson the students will explore the history of the Reformation and how it reshaped the church and gave rise to new denominations, including The United Methodist Church.

The students will explore the disagreements that led up to the Reformation, key Reformation figures, and the ways in which the Reformation affected the trajectory of church history all the way to the present day.

Lesson Outline

SECTION	TOPIC	DURATION
Connect	Telephone Drawings	10 minutes
Explore	The Protestant Reformers	25 minutes
Reflect	Always Reforming	5 minutes
Create	Three More Theses	15 minutes
Next	At home, at school, and in your community	Ideas to try this week

Supply List

Connect: Telephone Drawings
❑ Slips of paper (7 for each student)
❑ Writing utensils

Explore: The Protestant Reformers
❑ Internet-capable devices such as smartphones and tablets
❑ Paper
❑ Writing utensils

Reflect: Always Reforming
❑ Dry-erase board or projector
❑ Student Guides
❑ Writing utensils

Create: Three More Theses
❑ Student Guides
❑ Writing utensils

Next
❑ Student Guides

- C O N N E C T -

Telephone Drawings 10 minutes

[**LEADER PREP:** Before the lesson, prepare slips of paper for the opening activity. You will need 7 slips of paper for each student. You may use sticky notes, or you can cut regular sheets of paper into 16 even sections. Also for this activity, students will need to be seated around a table so that they can write and draw.]

SAY: Last week, we went on a whirlwind tour of the first 1,500 years of Christian history. We talked about some of the key figures, what they believed, and the things they accomplished. However, we didn't discuss some of the problems. We didn't mention the mistakes and flaws that sprang up in the church over hundreds of years. To explore that idea a little further, we're going to play a game.

[Hand out 7 slips of paper to each student along with a writing utensil.]

SAY: Write your initials on the top corner of each of your seven slips of paper. Make it small! Then stack your papers. [Wait until students are done initialing each paper]. On the top piece of paper I want you to write a short sentence telling your favorite thing about going to church. It should just be a few words, short and sweet.

[Allow the students a minute to write out their sentence.]

SAY: Once you've written your sentence, pass your stack of papers to the person on your left. They will silently read your sentence, then place that slip of paper at the bottom of the pile. Now, it's their job to draw a picture of the sentence that you wrote.

[Allow the students a minute to draw a picture of the sentence they received.]

SAY: Pass the stack of papers to your left again. Look at the picture. Move the slip of paper to the bottom of the pile, then write a sentence explaining what the picture means.

[The students will continue this process, alternating between drawing and writing, until all of the slips of paper have been used. Then they will pass the stack of papers to the person who wrote the original sentence.]

SAY: Do any of you want to share how the meaning of your sentence changed and shifted during the course of the game?

[Ask three or four students to share.]

SAY: Over hundreds and hundreds of years something similar to this happened to the church as well. As each generation passed the faith on to the next, meanings, beliefs, and practices inevitably shifted. Sometimes it was intentional, but often it was accidental like the way your sentence changed as it was passed around the room. These changes weren't necessarily good or bad, but some were quite significant and caused major problems and controversies in the church when people disagreed about how to understand the Christian faith.

At the highest level, these major problems and controversies, these shifts, are what lead to the period we call the Reformation.

- E X P L O R E -
The Protestant Reformers 25 minutes

[Divide the students in four groups of equal size. Make sure each group has paper and at least one student with a smartphone or tablet so that they can do research on the Internet. Also, make sure all of the students have a pen or pencil to take notes on what they discover in their research.]

SAY: When the church first started after Jesus' resurrection and ascension, it faced a lot of persecution. It was largely made up of poor and powerless people, and it also presented a political obstacle to the ruling Roman Empire. As time passed, the church continued to grow and became more powerful. The persecutions ended and Christianity was eventually named as the official religion of Rome.

This meant that, far from being persecuted, many Christians, including many Christian leaders, were now in positions of privilege. The church became a powerful player in politics and also grew extremely wealthy. When the Roman Empire eventually fell, the church helped to fill the vacuum of power.

Over time, the power and wealth of the church came into conflict with a number of groups that wanted change. These groups and their leaders believed that the church had lost its way and shifted too far from Jesus' original message. They wanted to redirect the church to the path they believed Jesus had intended. This was not the first group with such ideas, but this time their message was amplified by the invention of the printing press, which allowed books, essays, and pamphlets to be printed and widely distributed for the first time. Today, we are going to investigate four of the men who played a significant role in the Protestant Reformation. Each group will quickly research and make a short three-minute presentation about how each of the following leaders played an important role in the Reformation: Martin Luther, Thomas Cranmer, John Calvin, and Jacob Arminius. Your presentation can be anything from a short play to a song to a quick PowerPoint presentation. Be creative with what you learn!

[Assign each of the four groups one of the Reformers mentioned. Give the groups 10 minutes to research the person they are assigned. Walk around the room providing assistance while the groups do their research. If you have enough volunteers, place one with each group to aid them. When there are 2 minutes remaining, remind the students to prepare their quick presentation.]

SAY: Let's have our first group come up and tell us what they've learned about Martin Luther.

[Limit the presentations to 3 minutes. Use the summaries provided on page 62 to correct or fill in any important information that may have been left out. Continue on to the next presentations in the following order: Thomas Cranmer, John Calvin, and Jacob Arminius.]

SAY: These men and the movements they led have shaped the church immensely over the past 500 years; and their influence is still being felt today, including within The United Methodist Church.

- R E F L E C T -
Always Reforming 5 minutes

[**LEADER PREP:** Either write on the board or project the following saying in Latin and in English: "*Ecclesia semper reformanda est*" = "The church is always to be reformed." — Augustine]

SAY: Those words are attributed to Augustine; but over the centuries, scholars and church leaders have used them as a way to explain that the work of the church is never done. The church is always in pursuit of holiness, always striving toward its ultimate goal. In The United Methodist Church, we pursue this goal by using Scripture, tradition, reason, and experience, which is referred to as the Wesleyan Quadrilateral. We'll get into more detail about the Quadrilateral in the weeks to come, but it's important to mention today because it's the way Methodists think theologically about the direction of the church.

Today I want to invite you to think about what it means to be a church that is always reforming, always in pursuit of truth and holiness.

Write your answers to the following questions (from the Student Guide):

• What, do you think, does it mean that the church is always to be reformed?

• Why, do you think, is this important?

- C R E A T E -
Three More Theses 15 minutes

SAY: Who'd be willing to read aloud the instructions for the Create activity in your Student Guide?

  [Ask the volunteer to read the instructions.]

SAY: Take about 10 minutes to complete this activity. Go!

  [Allow time for the students to work on their own.]

SAY: Let's come back together and share our creations.

Discussion Questions As Time Allows

• Who'd be willing to share what you created?

• What did you like about this activity? What was challenging?

• What did you learn today that will stay with you?

- N E X T -

Ideas to Try This Week

[Point out the ideas to try during the week.]

At home: Choose someone from the list of people in the Explore section. Go online and look up even more information about him until you find something that you don't think your pastor or confirmation leader knows about this person. Share it with them at your next confirmation class.

At school: The Reformation reminds us God works through ordinary and everyday people. Talk with your friends at school about the ways that God can work through you. Make a list of three things you can do to continue to bring the love of God to the people around you.

In your community: The Reformation reminds us that the church is reformed and always being reformed by God. Take a prayer walk around your neighborhood, reflecting on the ways God is continuing to move in your community. How is God inviting you to be a part of this movement?

REFORMER SUMMARIES

Martin Luther

- German theologian, professor, priest, and monk
- He sparked the Reformation with the posting of the Ninety-Five Theses in Wittenberg, Germany.
- The theses were a call for a public debate on the church's usage of indulgences, a method where the church granted forgiveness of sins for a monetary gift.
- This became a larger conversation about the authority of the church and led to Luther's excommunication by Pope Leo X.
- Luther believed that salvation could not be earned through good deeds, but was only given by God's grace through faith.
- Luther believed that the Bible was only source of knowledge about God, and translated the Bible into German, making it more accessible to the common people.
- Every Protestant reformer, and every Protestant denomination was inspired in some way by Martin Luther.

John Calvin

- French theologian and reformer, most of his well-known work was done while serving in Geneva
- Heavily influenced by Augustine, he wrote a systematic theology called Institutes of the Christian Religion.
- He advocated the absolute sovereignty of God and that salvation and faith could only be granted by the grace of God, not through the act of free will.
- His theology also discussed political topics like how to organize and run a city and his work in Geneva put many of these practices into place.
- His theological beliefs, often referred to as Calvinism, are still very influential in many Presbyterian, Reformed, and Baptist congregations.

Jacob Arminius

- Dutch professor of theology
- He is most well known for his criticisms of Calvinist theology and advocacy for the importance of free will.
- He emphasized that salvation required believers to choose to believe, and that salvation and God could be both accepted and rejected.
- He introduced the idea of "prevenient grace," the idea that God's graceful action precedes human decisions, and exists without them needing to do anything to receive it.
- He is especially important for United Methodists because he heavily influenced the theology of John Wesley, who adopted his views on free will and prevenient grace.

Thomas Cranmer

- The father of the English Reformation
- He became the Archbishop of Canterbury under Henry VIII and Edward VI.
- Was a key figure in the Anglican Church's separation from the Catholic Church
- He created the first doctrinal and liturgical structure for the Church of England.
- He wrote the Book of Common Prayer, which is still used, with revisions, in the Anglican Church.
- Heavily influenced by Martin Luther's beliefs and reforms
- He died as a martyr when Queen Mary I (Bloody Mary), a Roman Catholic, took the throne after Edward VI.
- (Cranmer is particularly important because the Methodist movement emerges from the Anglican Church.)

Lesson

 8 *Wesley and the Methodists*

LESSON DESCRIPTION: In this lesson, the students will learn about John Wesley's personal history and how it influenced him to start the Methodist movement. They will also learn about how that movement grew, spread to the United States, and became a new denomination called the Methodist Episcopal Church.

Lesson Outline

SECTION	TOPIC	DURATION
Connect	Fake Out	15 minutes
Explore	Wesley and Friends	20 minutes
	Lesson 8 video: "Wesley and the Methodists"	5 minutes
Reflect	But What Does It Mean?	10 minutes
Create	A Methodist Timeline	15 minutes
Next	At home, at school, and in your community	Ideas to try this week

Supply List

Connect: Fake Out
❏ Slips of paper or sticky notes
❏ Writing utensils
❏ Small prizes such as candy

Explore: Wesley and Friends
❏ Lesson 8 video: "Wesley and the Methodists"

Reflect: But What Does It Mean?
❏ Student Guides
❏ Writing utensils

Create: A Methodist Timeline
❏ Student Guides
❏ Writing utensils

Next
❏ Student Guides

- C O N N E C T -

Fake Out 15 minutes

[**LEADER PREP:** Before the class begins, prepare slips of paper or sticky notes. There should be enough pieces for each student to have one. Also, be sure to have small prizes (candy or something similar) that you can give to people who win this game. Also, write out the correct answers on four more slips of paper that you will give to the readers at the appropriate time.]

Answers

The Christmas Conference: The first General Conference that founded the Methodist Episcopal Church. It was held in Baltimore, Maryland.

The Aldersgate Experience: The moment when John Wesley felt his heart "strangely warmed" by God. Occurred at a meeting on Aldersgate Street in London.

Holy Club: Group started by John and Charles Wesley at Oxford where members dedicated themselves to living a holy life.

Circuit Riders: Ministers who rode around on horseback and preached to a lot of churches. Francis Asbury was one of the first circuit riders.

SAY: Over the last few weeks, we've been talking about the history of the church, but this week we're going to start focusing more specifically on the history of The United Methodist Church. Later in this lesson, we'll be exploring some key events from the founding of Methodism; but first we want to test your creativity.

[Divide the students into four groups. Hand out the slips of paper and writing utensils to students. If you have a small group, repeat this process for 3 of the 4 phrases and have the whole group write a fake answer for each phrase. In this situation, you should read the answers aloud.]

SAY: We're going to play a play a game about important moments in the founding of Methodism. Here's how to play:

First, I'm going to give each group a phrase that refers to something significant in Methodist history. Then, each member of the group is going to try and make up a short one- or two-sentence explanation about what that phrase is referring to. The goal of the game is to come up with a fake explanation that's convincing enough that your classmates will choose it instead of the real one.

[After everyone has written out fake explanations, one person from your group will read them along with the real answer aloud to the rest of the class. Then everyone will vote on what they think the real answer is. If you can get someone to choose your answer, you'll get [a piece of candy or a small prize].

SAY: Remember, the goal is to come up with something creative enough and realistic enough to make someone pick your answer instead of the real one. Hint: Since the phrases are about Methodist history, it'll be more believable if you use famous Methodists like John Wesley, Charles Wesley, or Francis Asbury in your fake answer.

[Go to each group and give them their significant phrase: The Christmas Conference, The Aldersgate Experience, Holy Club, Circuit Riders. Give the students one or two minutes to write out a fake answer.]

SAY: Now that you've created your fake answers, each group will choose a reader, who will collect all of the answers in the group. Then I'll give this student the real answer, have them shuffle the answers, then read out each of the group's answers, including the right one. After they've read all the answers, you'll each vote for which answer you think is the real one. If anyone votes for the fake answer you wrote, you'll get a prize.

[Repeat this for all four groups.]

SAY: It's really hard to explain something from your history when you know only the name, but not how it fits into the story. Now that we know a little bit more about these events let's see where they fit into the story of Methodism.

- E X P L O R E -

Wesley and Friends *20 minutes*

SAY: The founder of the Methodist movement was John Wesley, an English priest in the 1700s who focused a lot of his work on the ideas of holiness and God's grace. Let's learn a little bit more about John Wesley's story and what he believed.

Video Time 5 minutes

[Show the Lesson 8 video: "Wesley and the Methodists."]

ASK: What stood out to you from the video?

Discussion Questions

• If you could only remember one thing from that video, what do think would be most important?

• What questions does that video make you ask about John Wesley?

• Why, do you think, were John Wesley's methods so influential?

[Allow the students to respond to these questions for 2 or 3 minutes.]

SAY: I am going to tell a short story about how Methodism grew and spread to the United States. So, listen carefully; because after the story, we will discuss some of the details of what you heard.

The Methodist movement started by John Wesley kept spreading throughout England, Scotland, and Ireland. Eventually, some of those who had joined the movement decided to move to the United States in search of new opportunities. Two of those immigrants were a former preacher named Philip Embury and his cousin Barbara Heck.

One day, Barbara caught her cousin Philip playing cards and was furious with him. Gambling was strictly opposed to the concepts of holiness taught within the Methodist movement, and Barbara believed that the move to America was making Philip pay less attention to his faith. As a result, she insisted that he start preaching again, even if it was just to his own family. Philip took her advice and started a small gathering with just his family. More people began to attend the family gatherings. This group eventually became the first Methodist congregation in America.

Wesley heard about this growing Methodist movement in the United States and sent a lay preacher named Francis Asbury to help them organize and spread the movement further. Asbury started the practice of circuit riding, in which a preacher would ride throughout the countryside preaching to a number of different societies that didn't have a dedicated minister.

Confirm Teaching Plans

Eventually, the Revolutionary War severed the ties between England and the United States. This was a particular problem for Methodist societies who were still technically part of the Church of England. All of the pastors in these congregations were ordained in the Church of England. This meant that many of the people who pastored American churches returned to England, leaving churches in a crisis about who would lead.

In response, Wesley ordained and sent Thomas Coke to be a superintendent of the Methodist societies. Coke, Asbury, and others traveled to Baltimore, Maryland, on December 24, 1784, to meet together and organize this new American church that would be separate from the Church of England. This meeting became known as The Christmas Conference and was the first General Conference of the newly formed Methodist Episcopal Church.

ASK: What do you think are the most important parts of this story? What questions do you have that you would like to learn answers to?

> [Have students brainstorm a few questions. Invite them to discuss these questions with their mentors and possibly investigate the answers together.]

SAY: Next week we'll explore more about how the Methodist Episcopal Church that started after the Revolutionary War became The United Methodist Church we're a part of today.

- R E F L E C T -

But What Does It Mean? *10 minutes*

SAY: Today you've been given a lot of information about how the Methodist movement began, about how it came to the United States, and about it eventually became a church independent from the Church of England. But you might be asking yourself, why is this important?

I could stand here and tell you why it's important, but I'd like to hear you answer that question yourself. Spend the next few minutes and write out why you think it's important that we learn about the origins of Methodism.

> [Give the students a few minutes to write in their journals. Invite students to share what they wrote with their neighbor and discuss their answers.]

- C R E A T E -

A Methodist Timeline 15 minutes

SAY: Who'd be willing to read aloud the instructions for the Create activity in your Student Guide?

[Ask the volunteer to read the instructions.]

SAY: Take about 10 minutes to complete this activity. Go!

[Allow time for the students to work on their own.]

SAY: Let's come back together and share our creations.

Discussion Questions

As Time Allows

• Who would be willing to share what you created?

• What did you like about this activity? What was challenging?

• What did you learn today that will stay with you?

- N E X T -

Ideas to Try This Week

[Point out the ideas to try during the week.]

At home: Write a short story about someone you learned about from the history of the Methodist church. Share your story with someone from your family.

At school: Hold your own "Holy Club" with your friends before or after school. What will you read? What will you talk about? What can your Holy Club do to make your school a better place?

In your community: Look up all the Methodist churches in your neighborhood. Send them a message online or stop by for a visit and ask them what it means to them to be a Methodist church.

Lesson

9 The Growth of Methodism

LESSON DESCRIPTION: This lesson will focus on the growth and development of the Methodist movement and the founding of The United Methodist Church. It will explore the history of the church in the United States from the time immediately after Thomas Coke and Francis Asbury through the Civil War and twentieth century until the beginning of the modern church. It will focus on important moments in church history and important social changes in the church during that time.

Lesson Outline

SECTION	TOPIC	DURATION
Connect	Most Important Moment	15 minutes
Explore	The United Methodists	20 minutes
Reflect	Three Questions	10 minutes
Create	A Snapshot of History	15 minutes
Next	At home, at school, and in your community	Ideas to try this week

Supply List

Connect: Most Important Moment
❑ Sheet of flip chart paper
❑ Sticky notes (5 per student)
❑ Writing utensils

Explore: The United Methodists
❑ A copy of the "United Methodist History Cards" cut along the dashed lines
❑ Scissors
❑ Internet-capable devices, such as smartphones and tablets

Reflect: Three Questions
❑ Student Guides
❑ Writing utensils

Create: A Snapshot of History
❑ Student Guides
❑ Writing utensils

Next
❑ Student Guides

- C O N N E C T -

Most Important Moment 15 minutes

[**LEADER PREP:** Place one piece of flip chart paper on the wall of the room and hand out five sticky notes to each student in the class. Label the paper "My Important Moments." As the students come in, direct them to think about the most important, most formative moments in their lives, the moments that stick out to them vividly.]

SAY: For our opening activity today, I want you to think about what makes you who you are. What events, what moments, what experiences have helped to shape who you've become, helped shape your passions, your hopes, your dreams. Maybe it was the first time you rode a bike or your first day of school. Using the sticky notes you've been given, write down the five most important moments of your life so far. Focus on the moments that have shaped you.

[Give the students three or four minutes to write down their answers.]

SAY: When you've finished writing your answers, go ahead and place your sticky notes on the piece of paper on the wall.

[After they've posted all their answers, read four or five aloud to share with the rest of the class.]

SAY: We all have these important moments. I'm sure that you'll have many more as you grow up, graduate from school, and go about the rest of your lives. I'm sure your parents have had these experiences too; maybe they've even shared them with you. Can any of you tell me about one of the most important experiences your parents or grandparents have ever told you about?

[Let a few students share, if they don't feel comfortable, be prepared, or have a volunteer prepared, to share one or two personal stories.]

SAY: Institutions have these stories too. The United States has stories about the Declaration of Independence, the Emancipation Proclamation, and the moon landing; stories that tell the story about who we are as a nation. The church has these stories too. We've talked in past few weeks about Augustine, the Reformation and John Wesley's Aldersgate experience.

Confirm Teaching Plans

This week we're going to focus specifically on the stories that have shaped The United Methodist Church into what it is today. And as we tell these stories today, remember that they aren't just the stories of The United Methodist Church; they are our stories as well. They are part of our history.

- E X P L O R E -

The United Methodists 20 minutes

[**LEADER PREP:** Make a copy of the "United Methodist History Cards," included in this lesson; and cut them into individual cards so that two cards can be given to each group.]

[Break your students up into 5 equal groups. If you have a smaller class, have the students partner up into as many groups as possible. Each group will be researching questions about United Methodist history together, so make sure each group has access to a smartphone or tablet.]

SAY: There are a lot of stories and events that went into the formation of The United Methodist Church. Just like your moments, some of these stories are powerful moments that the church wants to remember and some of them are moments that we'd rather forget. It's important, though, that we remember the good and the bad so that we can keep doing good and remember the consequences of when we do something bad.

Each group is going to be given two cards with a short explanation of something important in United Methodist history. Each card also has a question at the bottom. Read each card, then search online together to answer the question.

Check with the leader once you think you've answered your question to confirm that you're correct. Once you've found the answers to the questions on both of your cards, create a short creative way to explain the cards and answers to your classmates. You might use charades or a poem or even a short skit. You'll have 30–45 seconds to explain each card to the class.

[Distribute the cards to the class. Try to distribute the cards evenly so each group gets a question from two different parts of United Methodist history. Give the groups approximately 5 minutes to look up their answers and plan their presentations. Circulate around the room and check the answers of the students to make sure they are finding the correct answers. The correct answers are listed below.]

SAY: We're going to tell the story of The United Methodist Church in order so let's start with "Methodists on the Frontier."

[Continue in numerical order. Give each group 30–45 seconds for their creative explanation.]

Answers for the "United Methodist History Cards"

1. Circuit Riders

2. The African Methodist Episcopal Church, The African Methodist Episcopal Church Zion, and The Christian Methodist Episcopal Church

3. The Evangelical United Brethren

4. 1844

5. 1939

6. The Central Jurisdiction (**Leader:** For more information on the Central Jurisdiction and the story of race relations in the Methodist Church, visit *http://youthministrypartners.com/confirm.*)

7. Maud Keister Jensen (**Leader:** For more information, visit *http://umc.org/who-we-are/timeline-of-women-in-methodism.*)

8. The Social Principles

9. *Lay* means "someone who is not ordained." To become a layperson in The United Methodist Church, someone must be baptized and confirmed.

10. 122 (As of September 2016, lists of these schools are available here: *http://www.umc.org/directory/schools-seminaries.*)

- R E F L E C T -

Three Questions *10 minutes*

SAY: We just went through a lot of information about the history of The United Methodist Church and it can be a little bit overwhelming to take all of that in at once. Because of that, I want you to have a chance to process what you've just learned and focus on identifying the most important things that you heard. There are 3 questions in your Student Guide to help you focus on what you found most important. Go ahead and take five or six minutes to answer those and then we'll all discuss what you learned.

[Give the students 5 or 6 minutes to answer the questions. Walk around the room as they do; and every 2 minutes or so, remind the students to move on to the next question.]

SAY: Who'd like to share what you learned about Methodist history that you didn't know before?

[Allow two or three students to share.]

SAY: And what was the most surprising thing you found out?

[Allow two or three students to share.]

SAY: Now that you've heard about these parts of United Methodist history, what do you want to know more about? What questions do you have?

[Allow four or five students to ask questions, then invite them and the rest of the class to try to find those answers with their mentor this week.]

- C R E A T E -

A Snapshot of History 15 minutes

SAY: Who'd be willing to read aloud the instructions for the Create activity in your Student Guide?

[Ask the volunteer to read the instructions.]

SAY: Take about 10 minutes to complete this activity. Go!

[Allow time for the students to work on their own.]

SAY: Let's come back together and share our creations.

Discussion Questions *As Time Allows*

• Who would be willing to share what you created?

• What did you like about this activity? What was challenging?

• What did you learn today that will stay with you?

- N E X T -

Ideas to Try This Week

[Point out the ideas to try during the week.]

At home: Ask your parents or guardians why they choose to be a part of a Methodist church. Is it a part of your family heritage? Because they had friends at the church? Were there other factors that influenced this decision? Then ask them what they know about the history of the Methodist Church (and be sure to share a few things that you have learned).

At school: Find some friends from your confirmation class and issue a Church History Challenge. Go back and forth sharing things you remember about the history of the Methodist Church. Whoever can think of more things to share is the Church History Champion.

In your community: Walk around your church property and pay attention to the areas the church has grown and expanded into. Have there been any building renovations? A new parking lot? Fresh landscaping? Look for a cornerstone on the building that has a date of the church's construction. To learn even more, talk with a pastor at the church and have him or her tell you about the history and growth of your local Methodist church.

UNITED METHODIST HISTORY CARDS

Photocopy the cards and cut them out along the dashed lines.

1. Methodists on the Frontier

As the frontier went West, so did Methodism. Preachers who rode on horseback to many churches and towns went with the pioneers. They preached, held revivals, started classes, and planted new churches in almost every new town. Methodist pastors and Methodist churches seemed to be everywhere. Francis Asbury was among the first of these preachers, but he was far from the last.

What was the name given to these preachers who rode around from church to church and town to town?

2. African-American Methodist Churches

In the 1800s, as our country struggled with slavery, numerous African American Methodists experienced discrimination in The Methodist Episcopal Church. Many broke off and started their own Methodist denominations. These churches still exist. They are separate denominations but still part of our Methodist family. In numerous ways, these denominations and The United Methodist Church work together. Together they are called Pan-Methodists.

What are the names of the three denominations created by African American Methodists in the 1800s?

Answers for United Methodist History Cards

1. Circuit Riders
2. The African Methodist Episcopal Church, The African Methodist Episcopal Church Zion, and The Christian Methodist Episcopal Church
3. The Evangelical United Brethren
4. 1844
5. 1939
6. The Central Jurisdiction (**Leader:** For more information on the Central Jurisdiction and the story of race relations in the Methodist Church, visit *http://youthministrypartners.com/confirm.*)
7. Maud Keister Jensen (**Leader:** For more information, visit *http://umc.org/who-we-are/timeline-of-women-in-methodism.*)
8. The Social Principles
9. *Lay* means "someone who is not ordained." To become a layperson in The United Methodist Church, someone must be baptized and confirmed.
10. 122 (As of September 2016, lists of these schools are available here: *http://www.umc.org/directory/schools-seminaries.*)

3. German Methodists

During the early years, as Methodism was getting organized, there were numerous German-speaking people who were Methodists. Mainly due to language reasons, they did not join The Methodist Episcopal Church. Instead, they formed their own churches: The Evangelical Association and the United Brethren in Christ. Later these churches united and formed a new church. In 1968, this new church united with The Methodist Church, creating The United Methodist Church.

What was the name of the new church created by The Evangelical Association and the United Brethren in Christ?

4. The Church Splits

In the years leading up to the Civil War, the church split into three major denominations. First, The Methodist Protestant Church broke off over several issues, including the role of laypersons and bishops. Then, several years before the Civil War, the church split over slavery, becoming a northern church (The Methodist Episcopal Church) and a southern church (The Methodist Episcopal Church, South).

In what year did the church split into a northern church and a southern church?

5. The Church Reunites

After the end of the Civil War it took a long time for the three branches of Methodism that had split apart before the war to come back together. When they did, they formed The Methodist Church. Then, in 1968, The Evangelical United Brethren Church and The Methodist Church united to form The United Methodist Church.

In what year did the three branches of Methodism reunite to form The Methodist Church?

6. Segregation in the Church

After the three branches of Methodism reunited to form The Methodist Church in 1939 they arranged the annual conferences into five jurisdictions based on geography. However, they also segregated the black churches into a separate jurisdiction totally unrelated to the geographical location of the church. Black Methodists rightly saw the creation of this segregated jurisdiction as a betrayal and contrary to the mission of The Methodist Church and movement. But change did not come quickly. In 1956 the Church softened their policy, but the segregated jurisdiction was not eliminated entirely until the merger with the Evangelical United Brethren Church in 1968.

What was the name of the jurisdiction created by The Methodist Church to keep black churches segregated?

7. Women

Women played a vital role in the Methodist movement from the very beginning. Susanna Wesley, John and Charles's mother, was the primary religious influence in their early life. John Wesley even permitted women as lay preachers, a move that was both uncharacteristic and controversial for his time. In 1889, the United Brethren in Christ ordained a woman as a pastor. Years later, in 1956, The Methodist Church became the first large denomination to ordain women as clergy. Women were also vitally important in missions and social justice work in the late 1800s and early 1900s.

Who was the first woman to be ordained as clergy in The Methodist Church?

8. Social Justice

From the very beginning, the Wesleys and the other early Methodists were involved in the social issues of their day. They visited in prisons and jails, they cared for the sick, they opposed slavery, and they fought to keep children from working in the coal mines. As society changes, new issues emerge and The United Methodist Church continues to respond to these changing issues. For a church to take stands on controversial issues was surprising in 1908, when our church wrote its first Social Creed. But that is our tradition. We have always tackled controversial issues.

What is the name of the document that outlines The United Methodist Church's position on different social issues?

9. Lay Leadership

From the beginning, laypersons were key to the Methodist movement. Wesley was an ordained priest in the Church of England, but he could get few other pastors to join him in the movement. What he did find were lots of eager laypeople. Lay preachers and lay leaders gave the movement its momentum. Today, General Conference, the governing body of our denomination, is 50 percent laypersons and 50 percent ordained clergy in membership. Laypersons have as much right as clergy to submit legislation and ideas to General Conference. In The United Methodist Church, all baptized persons are ministers. Some are ordained; but all are ministers of the gospel. You are a minister of the gospel.

What does the word *lay* mean in this context? What does someone need to do to become a layperson in The United Methodist Church?

10. Education

John Wesley was a scholar. He believed in education, in books, and in learning. From the beginning, Methodists started schools everywhere they went. Methodism was active in the Sunday school movement in the 1700s, originally started to teach impoverished children to read. Today The United Methodist Church supports a number of colleges, universities, special schools, and seminaries.

How many educational institutions does The United Methodist Church support? Name three of them.

Lesson
10 Living Together

LESSON DESCRIPTION: This lesson will explore the history of your individual congregation and the students' relationship to the local church. The lesson will be focused on the experiences of the students in the church, the history of the church, and how the local church fits into the narrative of the church's longer history and heritage. It will highlight the particular historical tradition of your congregation and try to place this within the scope of the history of the church as explored in this unit.

Lesson Outline

SECTION	TOPIC	DURATION
Connect	What Is Your Story?	10 minutes
Explore	Where We Come From	20 minutes
Reflect	When We Gather	10 minutes
Create	Time-Traveling Letters	15 minutes
Next	At home, at school, and in your community	Ideas to try this week

Supply List

Connect: What Is Your Story?
❑ Pictures of your congregation throughout its history
❑ Slide show (optional)

Explore: Where We Come From
❑ Flip chart paper or a dry-erase board
❑ Markers
❑ Guest Speaker
❑ Pictures and or slide show (optional)

Reflect: When We Gather
❑ Flip chart paper or a dry-erase board with Matthew 18:20 written on it
❑ Student Guides
❑ Writing utensils

Create: Time-Traveling Letters
❑ Student Guides
❑ Writing utensils

Next
❑ Student Guides

Confirm Teaching Plans

- C O N N E C T -

What Is Your Story? *10 minutes*

[**LEADER PREP:** Decorate the walls of the room in historical photos of your local church. If you have access to one, a church library or a church historian could be invaluable in setting up the room. Otherwise, ask members of the congregation who have been around for many years to provide any photos they might have of the church 5, 10, or 20 years ago. Find the oldest pictures you can to accentuate the history of your local church.

If you can't post these pictures around the room, place them in a slide show and have the slide show running on a loop as the students enter the room and throughout the Connect activity.]

SAY: Over the last few weeks we've discussed the growth and development of the church as a worldwide institution, but today we're going to focus on this church in particular and how it came to be part of that larger story.

Before we get into the story of how this church began and how its changed over the years, let's talk about your personal story as part of this church.

[Invite the students to sit in a circle. If you have a group larger than 12, consider breaking them up into smaller discussion groups to facilitate conversation. Ask the students to respond to the following questions. Give them approximately 2 minutes to discuss each question.]

Discussion Questions

• What is your first memory of this church?

• Were you raised in this church? Have you attended other churches?

• How is this one different? How is it similar?

[Advise the students to focus on how the experiences of others in the class differ from their own. Remind them that all of these stories are part of the same story of your congregation.]

ASK: One final question: What do you know about the history of our church from before you attended?

[It is likely students will not know a lot about the history of your church. Allow the students to embrace the idea that they have much to learn about their church.]

- E X P L O R E -

Where We Come From 20 minutes

[**LEADER PREP:** In the weeks leading up to this lesson, ask someone from outside the confirmation program to prepare a 10- to 15-minute presentation on the history and founding of your particular congregation. If you have a church historian, he or she would be the perfect choice. Also consider asking the lead pastor (if he or she is not already involved in confirmation), or any member of the church who has been around for years and is willing to participate.

In preparation for this lesson, ask this person to include the following: the story about how the church was founded, the story of how the church got its name, any connections the church might have to historical moments or historical figures, a few stories about past members, former pastors, and their own experiences at the church. Also, ask the guest to discuss how he or she has been affected by the growth and development of the church. Encourage him or her to share pictures or slides as part of the presentation. These could be some of the pictures you use to decorate the room at the beginning of the lesson.]

SAY: In a few minutes, we'll have a special guest join our group to tell us more about the story of this church. Before that, let's brainstorm about things you want to learn about the church. What questions do you have?

[Allow the students two to three minutes to brainstorm questions about the history of your local church. Write these questions on either a large white piece of paper or a dry-erase board at the front of the room.]

SAY: These are great questions! Let's see if [guest's name] can help us find the answers to them.

[Introduce your guest speaker. Allow the speaker 10–15 minutes for the presentation.]

Confirm Teaching Plans

SAY: I'd like to give a round of applause to [guest's name] for joining us today and sharing about [his/her] experiences. Does anyone have any questions for [guest's name]?

[Invite the students to ask the questions they brainstormed at the beginning of the lesson, especially those questions that were left unanswered during the course of the presentation. If neither you nor the presenter know the answer, invite the student to research the answer for himself of herself.]

Discussion Question

• What one thing did you learn from this conversation that you didn't know before?

- R E F L E C T -

When We Gather *10 minutes*

[**LEADER PREP:** On a large white piece of paper or dry-erase board, write out Matthew 18:20, "For where two or three are gathered in my name, I'm there with them."]

SAY: Over the last 6 weeks, we've explored the history of faith and the history of the church. We've learned about people who came before us and how what they did affected our lives and our faith. I want you to spend the next 5 minutes focusing on what you've learned in the last few weeks and what it means to you in the context of this verse.

[Allow the students 5 to 7 minutes to reflect and journal about what they've learned in the past six weeks. As they write, occasionally interject reminders about what they've learned: the faith of Jesus, the development of the early church, the Reformation, John Wesley, the growth of Methodism.]

SAY: If any of you are comfortable sharing, I'd like to invite two or three of you to share your reflections with the class.

- CREATE -

Time-Traveling Letters 15 minutes

SAY: Who'd be willing to read aloud the instructions for the Create activity in your Student Guide?

[Ask the volunteer to read the instructions.]

SAY: Take about 10 minutes to complete this activity. Go!

[Allow time for the students to work on their own.]

SAY: Let's come back together and share our creations.

Discussion Questions As Time Allows

• Who'd be willing to share what you created?

• What did you like about this activity? What was challenging?

• What did you learn today that will stay with you?

- NEXT -

Ideas to Try This Week

[Point out the ideas to try during the week.]

At home: Talk with your parents or guardians at home about what church was like when they were kids. What has stayed the same? What has changed? And what do they think is coming next in the church?

At school: Find the teacher who has been at your school the longest and ask what he or she has learned from his or her time at the school. As you listen, how can you connect this teacher's experience at the school with someone's experience in the church?

In your community: Make some homemade greeting cards and write notes of encouragement to elderly or shut-in members of your church. It's important to connect with the whole church and not just the people who are the same age as you.

Unit 3: Our Life Together

In this unit, your group will jump with both feet into much of what makes the practice of United Methodism unique among Protestant denominations. We'll explore everything from how our church is organized to how we worship together! Youth will learn about the instrumental role our hymnal plays in preparing for worship, as well as what we believe about our practices of Holy Communion and baptism. The unit then provides an introduction to The United Methodist Social Principles, our guide to how to be United Methodists in our world. We close with a reminder that our understanding of social issues is meaningless unless we also take action on what we believe together! Your group will emerge from "Our Life Together" with not only a better understanding of our global church, but also a better understanding of what it means to be confirmed.

- CONTENTS -

Lesson

11 The Connection

LESSON DESCRIPTION: In this lesson, your group will explore some of the shape and function of the structure of The United Methodist Church.

Lesson Outline		
SECTION	**TOPIC**	**DURATION**
Connect	Game Time	15 minutes
	Unit 3 video: "Our Life Together"	5 minutes
Explore	A Brief History of Why	20 minutes
Reflect	I Feel You, Nehemiah	5 minutes
Create	Connect Them All	15 minutes
Next	At home, at school, and in your community	Ideas to try this week

Supply List

Connect: Game Time
- ❑ Several boardgames that involve moving game pieces around the board.
- ❑ Unit 3 video: "Our Life Together"

Explore: A Brief History of Why
- ❑ Bibles
- ❑ Posterboard
- ❑ Markers
- ❑ Paper and pen for each person

Reflect: I Feel You, Nehemiah
- ❑ Student Guides
- ❑ Writing utensils

Create: Connect Them All
- ❑ Student Guides
- ❑ Colored pencils or markers

Next
- ❑ Student Guides

Confirm Teaching Plans

- C O N N E C T -

Game Time *15 minutes*

[**LEADER PREP:** Set up several board games around the room. Games such as Sorry®, Parcheesi, or Monopoly® work well; but less familiar games may make the activity more interesting. Give preference to games that involve moving game pieces around the board.]

[Invite the youth to gather into groups around chosen games.]

SAY: What's the best way to learn how to play a game?

[Allow time for the group to respond.]

SAY: Take a few minutes to get familiar with the rules of the game you've gathered around. When you're done, we'll come back together and teach one another how each game is played.

[They don't have to memorize the rules, but a general grasp of game play is the goal. They're looking for things such as how many people can play, how the game begins, any special rules during play, and how the game concludes. When they're all comfortable with their understanding of their group's game, bring the whole group back together.]

SAY: Let's go around and share how each of our games is played.

[Invite the groups to demonstrate their game.]

• Why, do you think, is it important to understand how games are played?

• How would you play [name of a game] without knowing the instructions?

SAY: Today we're starting a new unit of *Confirm* called, "Our Life Together." Over the next few lessons, we'll be exploring some of the ways we uniquely approach things like worship, Communion, baptism, and how we should live in this world as United Methodists. Being Methodist is not about following certain rules; it is a community that has structure and activities that are connected and take on more meaning if we understand them. Being part of a church involves having common language for exploring faith and life together. Let's watch a short video about what we can expect from the next few weeks.

Video Time *5 minutes*

[Show the Unit 3 video: "Our Life Together."]

ASK: What stood out to you from the video?

- E X P L O R E -

A Brief History of Why 20 minutes

[After dividing your class into three groups, give each person a piece of paper and a pen, and each group a marker and posterboard.]

SAY: Number off in threes to form 3 groups.

[Allow the groups to form.]

SAY: As you listen to the story, I am about to read from the Bible, each of you will jot down bullet points from what you hear.

Group 1: You'll make a list of the actions in the story.

Group 2: Make a list with specifics of the issues that arise in the story.

Group 3: Make a list of the solutions that are provided in the story for the problems that arise.

After we are done with the story, you will combine your lists together on your group's posterboard. Are you ready to jump into the story?

SAY: Let me give you some background to our story for today. Most of the Old Testament focuses on a special community of people—described as "God's People"—also known as Hebrews or Israelites or Jews.

As you read through the Old Testament, you discover that this special group of people went through a lot. They were slaves in Egypt, led out by a courageous man named Moses. Then, they formed their own nation, appointing their own kings (sometimes with God's help). But they couldn't get along and didn't follow God's ways, so their kingdom split in two—a kingdom called Judah and a kingdom called Israel.

Israel was defeated by enemy nations and never really heard of again. The kingdom of Judah, with Jerusalem as its capital, was defeated by the Babylonians and taken into exile as a group.

Our story today picks up after some of the exiles returned to Jerusalem to find it in terrible condition. A man named Nehemiah was inspired to go to Israel and rebuild the walls that protected the city from enemies. He knew this would not be easy, as surrounding nations didn't want to see Judah become a kingdom once again. Let's pick the story now.

[Read or have a volunteer read aloud the story from Nehemiah 4.]

SAY: OK, combine your observations together on your poster board. You will also assign one person to share them with the group in a few minutes.

[After all 3 groups have written down their findings, have each group share them aloud.]

- R E F L E C T -

I Feel You, Nehemiah *5 minutes*

[Allow students time to reflect on this story in their Student Guides.]

Discussion Questions

• What did you notice in this story? In other words, what details stood out to you?

• What was new to you?

[Bring the 3 posters together.]

• Did we miss anything? How did your assignment affect how you listened to the story?

SAY: Both the boardgames we learned about earlier and Nehemiah's story showed the importance of structure and order.

• Where else in your life do you encounter structure that helps things work?

• Where do you sometimes find structure to be a little inhibiting?

• Where do you have opportunities to improve structure, or create it yourself?

- C R E A T E -

Connect Them All *15 minutes*

[Pairs of students will create mind maps connecting the seven components of the UMC. Make sure to find and print a sample mind map. Search for "simple mind map for students" and you should discover several useful images. As they create, ask them about each of the seven components, seeing what they know and sharing more information on each one. Research the seven components prior to class so you have something to share! For more information, visit *http://www.umc.org/who-we-are*.]

Discussion Questions As Time Allows

• What parts of the UMC did you know about before today's class? What new things did you learn about them?

• What parts of the UMC did you learn about for the first time today? What do you remember most about them?

• In your own words, what is the connection?

• Why is the connection important in the UMC?

• Describe a time you felt connected to a group or community.

• Describe a time you felt disconnected from a group or community.

- N E X T -

Ideas to Try This Week

[Point out the ideas to try during the week.]

At home: Go online and research more about the structure of the United Methodist Church. Visit www.umc.org/who-we-are to learn more about how the UMC is organized. Search online to see how many UMC churches you can find near you.

At school: Talk to a teacher or principal at your school and ask them about how the school is structured and how all the parts are connected. How does it compare with the structure and connection of The United Methodist Church?

In your community: Find the three nearest United Methodist churches (aside from the one you attend). Contact them, either in person, over the phone, or via e-mail. Introduce yourself to the pastor and thank them for being a part of "the connection."

Confirm Teaching Plans

Lesson

12 Simple Worship

LESSON DESCRIPTION: In this lesson, your group will explore the things that are important to the heart of United Methodist worship—and examine some of the things that often aren't. We pack a lot of things into our worship services; what is really essential in United Methodist worship? We'll look at our own practices of worship and dig into a story where a woman challenges Jesus about what true worship means and where it takes place.

Lesson Outline		
SECTION	**TOPIC**	**DURATION**
Connect	Picking Apart Worship	15 minutes
Explore	The Woman at the Well	10 minutes
Reflect	Defining Worship	5–10 minutes
Create	A New Way to Worship	15 minutes
Next	At home, at school, and in your community	Ideas to try this week

Supply List

Connect: Picking Apart Worship
- ❏ As many things as possible that are generally involved in standard practices of worship: candles, a Bible, copies of *The United Methodist Hymnal,* chairs or pews, a guitar, sheet music, a laptop, a projector, bread, grape juice, an elder, an order of service or bulletin, a sheet of announcements (or even someone making announcements), and anything else that crosses your mind
- ❏ Posterboard for groups to write their order-of-importance lists (optional)

Explore: The Woman at the Well
- ❏ Bibles
- ❏ Paper
- ❏ Writing utensils

Reflect: Defining Worship
- ❏ Student Guides
- ❏ Writing utensils

Create: A New Way to Worship
- ❏ Student Guides
- ❏ Writing utensils

Next
- ❏ Student Guides

- C O N N E C T -

Picking Apart Worship 15 minutes

[*LEADER PREP:* As you begin, point to or hold up items you've collected that are involved in standard practices of worship: candles, hymnals, chair/pews, guitars, a laptop and projector, a Bible, bread, grape juice, sheet music, an elder, an order of service or bulletin, a sheet of announcements, and so on. If any items are unfamiliar to the group, explain what role that item usually plays in a worship service.]

SAY: We're going to divide into two teams to do something that might seem unusual. Once we've divided, each team will be responsible for putting all of these items in order of importance in a worship service. Be prepared to defend your selections! If you think that the bread is more important than the grape juice you'd better have a reason. One more thing: no ties. You have to put everything in order.

[Divide the group into teams as you see fit. For larger groups, it may work better to divide into more than two teams. Try to avoid having more than 10 people on a team. When they've finished, allow time for the groups to present and defend the order they selected. Debrief with the questions below.]

Discussion Questions

• What was your process for deciding the order of importance for all of these things we use in worship?

• Why do we use each of these things in worship?

• How would your process have been different if, for example, you had to narrow the number of items down to five?

• How does our church determine what is necessary for worship?

- E X P L O R E -

The Woman at the Well 10 minutes

SAY: Jews and Samaritans didn't get along at all. After the northern kingdom of Israel was conquered by Assyria, outsiders—the

Confirm Teaching Plans

Samaritans—were brought in to care for the land. When Jews later returned to Jerusalem, they clashed—to say the least. Most of the time they would avoid one another altogether in public.

So it was incredibly unusual for a Jewish man (Jesus) to be speaking to a Samaritan woman, but that's exactly what happens in the story we're about to read. The woman in the story has been married several times, but we don't know what circumstances were involved. She recognizes the authority with which Jesus speaks, and proceeds to ask him a question about worship that will drive our discussion here.

[Hand out paper and writing utensils.]

SAY: Who'd be willing to read aloud John 4:1-24?

[Choose several volunteers to read.]

SAY: As each volunteer reads, write or sketch details that stand out to you from the story.

[Have the volunteers read and everyone write or sketch details.]

Discussion Questions

• What things did you write down or draw?

• What, do you think, does this story have to do with worship?

• What did the woman think was important about worship?

• What did Jesus suggest was more important about worship?

- R E F L E C T -

Defining Worship 5-10 minutes

[Students often associate the word *worship* with singing or a service time, such as 10 o'clock worship or 11 o'clock worship. Use this Reflect section to get them engaged in what is really meant to happen during worship.]

Discussion Questions

• We don't really put things in order of importance for worship, but when have you seen something highlighted as extra important during a service?

• When have you thought something was given too much importance?

• What about a time when you thought something was not given enough importance?

• What do you think is most important to God in our worship services?

• What from our list could be completely eliminated and still leave us with worship?

SAY: Partner with someone near you and spend two minutes coming up with a definition of *worship* to share with the group. Space is provided in your Student Guide.

[Allow about 2 minutes for them to reflect, then ask groups to share.]

- C R E A T E -

A New Way to Worship *15 minutes*

[Students will choose one of the four movements in worship (listed in their Student Guides) or a specific piece within one of those movements and design a new and creative way to experience it in your church's worship service. You may choose to make it optional for students to work with a partner.]

SAY: Who'd be willing to read aloud the instructions for the Create activity in your Student Guide?

[Ask the volunteer to read the instructions for the Create activity.]

SAY: Take about 10 minutes to complete this activity. Go!

[Allow 10 minutes for the students to work on their own.]

SAY: Let's come back together and share our creations.

Discussion Questions *As Time Allows*

• Why did you select the area (movement) you chose?

• Did you have ideas for other movements? What are they?

• Why, do you think, is it hard for church leaders to come up with creative ways to worship?

• How could we help them?

- N E X T -

Ideas to Try This Week

[Point out the ideas to try during the week.]

At home: In the Create section, you redesigned one part of a worship service. Why not redesign the whole thing? Use your creativity to come up with a complete worship service. Make sure it includes all four movements (Entrance, Proclamation and Response, Thanksgiving and Communion, Sending Forth). Bring your ideas to the next confirmation class and show them to your pastor or confirmation instructor.

At school: A United Methodist worship service has four intentional movements. Chances are your typical school day does too. Track the rhythms and movements of a day at school. What would you call each one? What purpose do they serve? How do you experience your day differently when you are aware of the "liturgy" of your day? How do you experience worship on Sunday morning differently when you are more aware of the order of service?

In your community: The final movement of the United Methodist worship liturgy is Sending Forth, to enter the world and discover and join the movement of God. Wake up early and take a walk around your neighborhood. Where do you notice God at work? Take the same walk again, this time in the evening. Where do you notice God at work? What do you notice God calling you to do?

Lesson
13 Music and Lyrics

LESSON DESCRIPTION: In this lesson, your group will explore and engage the rich resource that is our *United Methodist Hymnal*. Our hymnal provides not only hymns for all the seasons of the church year and various Wesleyan theological themes, but also orders of service for many different events in the life of the church.

Lesson Outline		
SECTION	TOPIC	DURATION
Connect	Get Packing	15 minutes
Explore	Paul's Dress Code	10 minutes
	Lesson 13 video: "Music and Lyrics"	5 minutes
Reflect	A Song to Sing	5–10 minutes
Create	Move Over, Charles Wesley!	15 minutes
Next	At home, at school, and in your community	Ideas to try this week

Supply List

Connect: Get Packing
❏ Large suitcase
❏ Several sets of clothing representative of different seasons (bathing suits and down jackets, snow boots and flip-flops, for example). The more clothes the better, and the more complete head-to-toe outfits the better. Be sure not to set them out in outfits, but rather mix them together. Ideally the youth will arrive to see a jumbled mess of clothing.
❏ Accessory clothing items: ball caps, neckties, sunglasses a beach ball, sunscreen, and the like to help fill out the activity
❏ Drawing paper
❏ Writing utensils

Explore: Paul's Dress Code
❏ Bibles
❏ Internet-capable devices such as smartphones and tablets
❏ Paper
❏ Writing utensils
❏ Lesson 13 video: "Music and Lyrics"

Reflect: A Song to Sing
❏ Copies of *The United Methodist Hymnal*
❏ Writing utensils

Create: Move Over, Charles Wesley!
❏ Copies of *The United Methodist Hymnal*
❏ Student Guides
❏ Writing utensils

Next
❏ Student Guides

Confirm Teaching Plans

- C O N N E C T -

Get Packing *15 minutes*

[**LEADER PREP:** Place a large suitcase in the middle of the group. Surrounding the suitcase should be a jumbled mess of clothing and accessories (see supply list).]

SAY: Today we're packing for a special trip—but first of all, we've got a little bit of a mess to clean up. Let's organize these clothes by type. Put the pants with other pants, shorts with shorts, and so on.

[Give the students a few minutes to sort out the clothes pile.]

SAY: Now that we've got things a little better organized, we can pack for our trip. Who will volunteer to pack for a trip to the beach?

[Choose someone and allow him or her to pack.]

While they pack, everyone else may draw on a sheet of paper something that you always seem to forget when packing for warm weather.

SAY: How did you decide what to bring?

[Empty the suitcase again.]

SAY: OK, now it's Christmas, and we're headed to the mountains for skiing. What should we pack?

[Have another volunteer pack the suitcase for a winter trip.]

The rest of you can draw next to your warm weather drawing a winter item that you were perpetually losing when you were a little kid.

ASK: How would your travel be different if you only had one season of clothing to put in your suitcase? What challenges would you face if you had to pack out of a huge, disorganized pile every time you were headed out of town?

- E X P L O R E -

Paul's Dress Code *10 minutes*

SAY: A big part of why Christians come together in the local church is the ability to help one another grow spiritually. If we're sharing life, we're more likely to be willing to listen to advice from one another about

Lesson 13

how we're living life. That closeness also gives us better opportunities to observe and learn from the lives of others.

That's what the apostle Paul is talking about when he tells the church at Colossae to put on compassion, kindness, humility, gentleness, and patience. The NIV actually translates this as "clothe yourselves"! Just like with the suitcase a moment ago, we can use each other's help picking out our "spiritual" clothing.

Today we're talking about our *United Methodist Hymnal*. Let's spend a few minutes finding the places in Scripture where we're encouraged to come to God in song. You can use the concordance at the back of your Bible or the Internet to search for the words *hymn, song,* and *praise* in Scripture. Share with your neighbor your favorite of the Scriptures you find.

> [Give the students several minutes to search and write, then bring them back together.]

ASK: Who'd like to share what you found?

> [Allow a few youth to share.]

SAY: Let's go back to Paul in Colossians. Someone, please read for us Colossians 3:8-16.

> [Ask a volunteer to read aloud.]

Discussion Questions

• What, do you think, is Paul instructing the Colossians to do?

> [Read verse 16 aloud again.]

• What is an example of something you've learned from a song?

SAY: The early church didn't have a hymnal anything like ours; they most likely were singing songs from Psalms, which served as their songbook for worship before the Christian movement grew into home churches. They were passing down songs and psalms of instruction from one generation to the next. Let's check out a video about the writer of dozens of the hymns in our *United Methodist Hymnal*, Charles Wesley.

Video Time *5 minutes*

[Show the Lesson 13 video: "Music and Lyrics."]

ASK: What stood out to you from the video?

- R E F L E C T -

A Song to Sing *5-10 minutes*

SAY: Sometimes when we sing hymns—especially if they're familiar—we think more about the melody than the words. If we're meant to teach each other with hymns, however, the words mean more than the melody! Let's read a hymn written by the guy from the video we just watched, Charles Wesley. According to *UMDiscipleship.org*, this hymn is placed first in our hymnal to show its significance in our United Methodist tradition.

[Ask volunteers to take turns reading the verses of hymn 57, "O for a Thousand Tongues to Sing."]

Discussion Questions

• What, do you think, is the main thing the writer is trying to express?

• How often do you pay attention to the words of the songs we sing in church?

• Can you remember anything unusual you've ever heard in a song or hymn here?

• Anything you didn't understand?

SAY: The songs in the *United Methodist Hymnal* were carefully chosen from hundreds of years of hymns, selecting only those that agree with our United Methodist beliefs.

Spend a couple of minutes looking through the hymns, and write in your Student Guide a favorite lyric that you come across. Be sure to write down the hymn number so you can come back and look at it later.

- CREATE -

Move Over, Charles Wesley! *15 minutes*

SAY: Who would be willing to read aloud the instructions for the Create activity in your Student Guide?

[Ask the volunteer to read the instructions from the Student Guide.]

SAY: Take about 10 minutes to complete this activity. Go!

[Allow the students 10 minutes to work on their own.]

SAY: Let's come back together and share our creations.

[If time allows, let the group try to sing some of the new verses.]

Discussion Questions *As Time Allows*

• What did you like about this activity?

• What was challenging?

• Why, do you think, are hymns so important to us as Methodists?

- NEXT -

Ideas to Try This Week

[Point out the ideas to try during the week.]

At home: Find a *United Methodist Hymnal* or go online and visit *hymnary. org/hymnal/UMH.* Browse through the hymns and make a list of your top five. Include your "old favorites" as well as new discoveries. Be sure to read the lyrics closely as you make your decisions. Then e-mail your top five hymns to your pastor or confirmation leader and a friend from your confirmation class, inviting them to send you their top five hymns.

At school: What is your school's fight song? Talk to the teachers and administration and find out what it is. What is the melody? What are the lyrics? What are they communicating about your school?

In your community: Pay attention to the music that you hear in your community. What do you hear on the radio, car stereos, and soundtracks to your favorite movies and TV shows? Make a list of all the songs you hear over the course of one day. Then journal about how these particular songs affect your experience of the day. What songs would you want as a part of your soundtrack? Why?

Lesson
14 Remembrance

LESSON DESCRIPTION: In this lesson, your group will explore the elements and significance of the United Methodist practice of Holy Communion. Holy Communion is one of two sacraments in The United Methodist Church, and we'll lean into what makes our understanding of it unique to us.

Lesson Outline

SECTION	TOPIC	DURATION
Connect	Bread, Wine, and Mystery	10 minutes
Explore	Diving in	10 minutes
Reflect	Celebrating Grace	5–10 minutes
Create	You're Invited!	15 minutes
Next	At home, at school, and in your community	Ideas to try this week

Supply List

Connect: Bread, Wine, and Mystery
❑ Three plates (paper or dinnerware)
❑ Large napkins or cloths to cover the plates
❑ Plain box (4-by-4 or smaller) that you write (or attach) question marks on
❑ Dinner roll or slices of bread.
❑ A bunch of grapes.
❑ Paper
❑ Writing utensils

Explore: Diving in
❑ Bibles
❑ Copies of *The United Methodist Hymnal*

Reflect: Celebrating Grace
❑ Student Guides
❑ Writing utensils

Create: You're Invited!
❑ Copies of *The United Methodist Hymnal*
❑ General art supplies: construction paper, glue, scissors, colorful tissue paper, markers, and so forth
❑ Student Guides
❑ Writing utensils

Next
❑ Student Guides

Confirm Teaching Plans

- C O N N E C T -

Bread, Wine, and Mystery *10 minutes*

[**LEADER PREP:** Prior to your group arriving, place three plates on a table. On the first, put a bunch of grapes. On the second, place a small cardboard box—no bigger than 4 inches square, ideally—with question marks drawn (or attached) all over it. On the third, place a dinner roll or a few pieces of bread. Cover all three plates with cloths before your group arrives.]

[After all of the students have arrived, hand out paper and writing utensils. Then uncover the first plate.]

SAY: Someone seems to have left us something to figure out. What are these for?

[Uncover the second plate to reveal the box.]

SAY: Well, that's odd.

[Look into the box.]

SAY: Nothing is in the box. What do you think this box represents? Take a moment to write down your guess on a piece of paper. Fold it and put it in your pocket; and in a minute, we'll see if anyone got it right.

[Uncover the third plate.]

SAY: Hmmm. Bread, grapes, and a box with question marks all over it. What do you think is going on here?

[Allow time for responses.]

SAY: Let's go around and share our guesses from a moment ago. What do you think the box represents?

[Let everyone share.]

SAY: "Questions" is a good guess, but it is something else.

Now, if we didn't have the strange little box here, what church thing would the grapes and bread make you think of?

[Here they should arrive at the answer: "Communion." If not, make the jump for them from grapes to grape juice.]

Lesson 14

SAY: The truth is, Communion is more than the bread and wine (or juice). It is also about mystery. That is what this box represents. The bread represents the body of Christ, and the grape juice the blood of Christ. The mystery is how God is present in these elements and present with us when we celebrate this meal together.

- E X P L O R E -

Diving In 10 minutes

SAY: Today we're learning about a sacrament of The United Methodist Church. A sacrament is an outward and visible sign of the inward working of grace. In The United Methodist Church, we practice two that were modeled in the life of Jesus. Can any of you name both?

> [The two sacraments are baptism and Communion. Baptism is in the next lesson.]

> [Divide the youth into three groups. Assign each group one of the Lord's Supper texts from Matthew 26:17-30; Mark 14:12-26; and Luke 22:7-20.]

SAY: In your groups, take a look at your assigned story. Have one person read aloud. Another can write down the details of how the supper Jesus shared with his disciples takes place. Pay special attention to the way the cup and bread are described and given.

Listen for specific words that are said by Jesus and the disciples.

All of you should help point out the details as they emerge in the story.

> [Invite each group to read aloud their version of the story to the entire group. When they've finished reading, allow the group to compare and contrast the slight differences among them.]

Discussion Questions

• What was the same from each version?

• What was unique from each version?

• Why, do you think, does Communion continue to be such an important part of our faith?

SAY: Communion offers us an opportunity to step together into the mystery of God. We remember Jesus' willingness to suffer and give his life. We remember his love for his disciples. We remember that we have the opportunity to offer ourselves in sacrifice to God, so that others might know God's love. But we also know that Christ is "present through the community gathered in Jesus' name . . . , through the Word proclaimed and enacted, and through the elements of bread and wine shared. The divine presence is a living reality and can be experienced by participants; it is not a remembrance of the Last Supper and the Crucifixion only" (*This Holy Mystery,* page 10). This is why we take Communion. It's a mystery we can't fully understand, which is why our elements (the bread and wine) and our liturgy for Communion remain constant so that no matter which United Methodist elder is presiding over Communion, our experience of Holy Communion remains consistent.

[If time allows, have a student read from the liturgy for Communion from *The United Methodist Hymnal.* Begin on page 11 with the second paragraph: "On the night in which he gave himself up for us . . ." and read up to the end of the section before The Lord's Prayer.]

- R E F L E C T -

Celebrating Grace 5–10 minutes

SAY: Communion happens many different ways across Christian churches. Some take it every day. Some once a week. Most United Methodists take it once a month, while other denominations participate only once a quarter—four times a year.

As United Methodists, we practice something called open table when we offer Communion. If a church or denomination considers its table closed, it means that they offer Communion only to people who are committed members in that faith tradition. Our open table welcomes anyone who feels drawn to it by God. We're not unique in this practice, but it is certainly a United Methodist distinction.

Discussion Questions

• How does this shared meal bring God's grace into our lives?

• How does it empower us to do God's work?

SAY: We come together in community around this meal to be renewed for our ministry in the world around us. The meal itself reminds us of how God's grace makes us whole—the justifying grace we have explored in previous lessons.

ASK: What does Communion mean to you?

[Allow several students to answer.]

SAY: Spend a couple of minutes answering the questions in your Student Guide.

[Allow the students 2 minutes to work on their own.]

- C R E A T E -

You're Invited 15 minutes

[The students will design two greeting cards, inviting themselves and someone else to celebrate Communion at church. They will use their Student Guide to sketch a mock-up of their card before making the real thing with various art supplies.]

ASK: Who'd be willing to read aloud the instructions for the Create activity in your Student Guide?

[Ask the volunteer to read the instructions in the Student Guide.]

SAY: Take about 10 minutes to complete this activity. Go!

[Allow the students 10 minutes to work on their own.]

SAY: Let's come back together and share our creations.

Discussion Questions *As Time Allows*

• What did you like about this activity? What was challenging?

• Why, do you think, did we made a card to ourselves? What might this help us think more deeply about?

• Do you think that it will be easy or awkward to invite someone to Communion? Why?

- N E X T -

Ideas to Try This Week

[Point out the ideas to try during the week.]

At home: Communion is about remembering. What objects or traditions do you have at home that help you remember? Are there photos on the wall? Family traditions that you do? Explore some of the ways you and your family remember the experiences you've had and the love that you share.

At school: Gather your friends from confirmation class and eat lunch together. As you share your meal together, talk more about the things you remember from this lesson about Communion. How does it feel to talk about this sacred meal during an ordinary one?

In your community: Talk with your family and then invite your neighbors over for a meal. The only purpose of this invitation is to get to know them better. Pay attention to where you notice God in the midst of the meal and your time together. How does this shared meal remind you of what you learned about Communion at church?

Lesson

15 Accepting Grace

LESSON DESCRIPTION: In this lesson, your group will explore the meaning and significance of baptism and confirmation. Your students will examine, in particular, how grace moves through those events. Best of all, it will show how they have the opportunity to receive the grace that already exists for them.

Lesson Outline

SECTION	TOPIC	DURATION
Connect	Looking Back	15 minutes
Explore	A Different Kind of Believer	10 minutes
Reflect	Making It Your Own	5–10 minutes
Create	Rising Grace	15 minutes
Next	At home, at school, and in your community	Ideas to try this week

Supply List

Connect: Looking Back
❑ Several uninflated balloons for each person
❑ 1 permanent marker for each person
❑ 1 inflated helium balloon

Explore: A Different Kind of Believer
❑ Bibles
❑ Helium balloon from the Connect activity

Reflect: Making It Your Own
❑ Student Guides
❑ Writing utensils

Create: Rising Grace
❑ Balloons from the Connect activity
❑ Uninflated balloon for each person
❑ Markers
❑ Half-sheets of paper
❑ Student Guides
❑ Writing utensils

Next
❑ Student Guides

Confirm Teaching Plans

- C O N N E C T -

Looking Back *15 minutes*

SAY: As we grow up, there are more and more things that we take responsibility for in our lives. We come into this world pretty vulnerable and unprotected, not to mention totally incapable of providing for ourselves. We rely on the adults around us—usually our parents, but sometimes other family or guardians—to provide for us until we are able to do so for ourselves.

ASK: What things did your parents once do for you that you now do for yourself?

[Give each person several uninflated balloons.]

SAY: As you think of something, inflate one of your balloons, tie it, and write that thing on it before placing it in a pile on the floor.

[In this first stage, they'll be looking for things like "fed me," "dressed me," "sheltered me," and the like. When you have a good number of balloons inflated and lying in the floor, move on to the next prompt.]

SAY: Now think of things your parents do that you haven't yet taken over from your them but will one day. As each one comes to you, inflate a balloon and write that thing on the balloon.

[These will be things like "drive me," "pay for my things," "provide for my education," and so on. When the pile of balloons has increased, move on.]

SAY: This has all been working toward talking about the presence of grace in our lives. Grace is a little different from the other things we've named so far. Your parents aren't responsible for grace being part of your life; that's the work of God. But your parents have the opportunity to recognize the presence of God's grace in your lives and even ask our congregation to join in helping raise you to recognize it for yourself. Because grace is different from all of these things, we'll present it slightly differently—it's the only balloon that will float on its own.

[Write the word *grace* in large letters on the helium balloon.]

SAY: We'll explore this more as today's session proceeds, but grace is one thing that our parents have the opportunity to recognize in our lives before we're old enough to understand it for ourselves.

Lesson 15   107

- E X P L O R E -

A Different Kind of Believer

10 minutes

SAY: The central character in the Scripture we will be exploring today is an "Ethiopian eunuch." A eunuch was a highly placed official who had been castrated to place him above reproach—no way there would be a sexual scandal from him. This man was a highly respected government official, but treated as an outcast by the Jewish people.

As an Ethiopian he is presented as a foreigner, an early indicator of God's intention that the gospel be presented to everyone. However, the fact that he's returning from worship at the Jerusalem Temple suggests some tie to Judaism—his family lineage may have been part of the diaspora when Israel and Judah were conquered some 400 years before Jesus' birth. The fact that he went even though he would not be admitted to the Temple shows the strength of his commitment to learning about God!

> [Have your group take turns reading the verses from Acts 8:26-39. Hand the helium balloon to the first reader. have them pass the balloon as they take turns When the reading is completed, tie the balloon to a chair to keep it in place for the rest of the session.]

Discussion Questions

• What, do you think, was the Ethiopian trying to understand? Why couldn't he understand it on his own?

• What role did Philip play in the Ethiopian coming to an understanding of the good news about Jesus?

• How, do you think, would the Ethiopian's story have been different if Philip hadn't come alongside him?

> [Don't let this response be as simple as, "he wouldn't know God." The Ethiopian was already engaged in worshiping God at the temple. Chances are likely that he would have eventually encountered another Christian. Make this about the opportunities we have to share our faith with others.]

- R E F L E C T -

Making It Your Own *5–10 minutes*

[The process of confirmation offers youth not only some grounding in the ways of United Methodism, but a very intentional opportunity to consider making a faith commitment of their own. To this point in their lives, their families, their church, and other invested individuals have engaged in their spiritual care, recognizing the movement of God's grace in and around them. Confirmation is the first time the church asks them, "Are you ready?" Remember, we're introducing the idea of commitment here; the final unit of Confirm revisits this in more tangible ways. But here we start the ball rolling.]

Discussion Questions

• What's your earliest memory of any awareness of God?

• Do you know whether you were baptized as an infant or a small child?

• How have your family and church introduced you to understanding God better—like Philip did with the Ethiopian?

• Why, do you think, do we go through confirmation at our church?

SAY: Now turn to your Student Guide and journal a response to the questions in the Reflect section.

- C R E A T E -

Rising Grace *15 minutes*

[Students will create thank-you notes and place them inside of balloons. Pass out another balloon, a marker, and a half-sheet of paper to each student.]

ASK: Who'd be willing to read aloud the instructions for the Create activity in your Student Guide?

[Ask the volunteer to read the instructions in the Student Guide.]

SAY: Take about 10 minutes to complete this activity. Go!

[Allow the students 10 minutes to work on their own.]

SAY: Let's come back together and share our creations.

Discussion Questions *As Time Allows*

• What did you like about this activity? What was challenging?

• How did you choose which thing you were most grateful for? Why does that thing mean so much to you?

• How has God shown you grace?

- N E X T -

Ideas to Try This Week

[Point out the ideas to try during the week.]

At home: One way to remember God's grace is by remembering your baptism. Create small signs that say "Remember your baptism!" and place them around every source of water in your home.

At school: Baptism is all about grace, and grace is all about gratitude. Write nine thank-you notes to teachers and friends at school for things that you are grateful for. Then write a tenth thank-you note to God. Open your Bible to the story of the Ethiopian official (Acts 8) as a reminder of the connection between baptism, grace, and gratitude.

In your community: The story of Philip and the Ethiopian official reminds us that the grace we receive in baptism brings together communities that might otherwise remain separate. Where are there separations between people in your community (race, class, religion, etc.)? What can you do to help connect with others in the midst of a cultural separation? How do you think you will experience God in something like this?

Lesson
16 A Loving Church

LESSON DESCRIPTION: In this lesson, your group will explore the Social Principles of The United Methodist Church. The Social Principles are the expression of the UMC's guidance for how we, the church, are to live in and engage our world with the love of God. This is a deep dive into the way The United Methodist Church thinks and expresses itself. Be sure to emphasize the process of how these principles came together.

SECTION	TOPIC	DURATION
	Lesson Outline	
Connect	New House Rules	15 minutes
Explore	All in the Details	10 minutes
	Lesson 16 video: "A Loving Church"	5 minutes
Reflect	What About . . . ?	5–10 minutes
Create	A Church Built on Love	15 minutes
Next	At home, at school, and in your community	Ideas to try this week

Supply List

Connect: New House Rules
❑ Markers
❑ Posterboard

Explore: All in the Details
❑ Bibles
❑ Lesson 16 video: "A Loving Church"

Reflect: What About . . . ?
❑ Copies of the Social Principles or *The Book of Discipline*
❑ Student Guides
❑ Writing utensils

Create: A Church Built on Love
❑ Student Guides
❑ Writing utensils

Next
❑ Student Guides

- C O N N E C T -

New House Rules 15 minutes

LEADER PREP: This Connect activity will explore how house rules generally come to be. We're connecting to Social Principles of The United Methodist Church, which is the body of content that reflects the official United Methodist take on social issues, both broadly and specifically. The Social Principles appear in *The Book of Discipline* but are also available as a standalone book. Having a basic familiarity with the Principles in either form will be helpful to your process of leading this session.

SAY: Share with a friend a household rule from your family that you find funny or unusual.

[It's unlikely, but be sensitive to any house rules that intimate the possibility of abuse. If something like that comes up, speak immediately with your pastor at the end of this session and be sure to know your local laws about reporting as well as your church's Safe Sanctuary policy.]

Discussion Questions

• Why, do you think, do you have rules in your family? in society?

• Have you ever helped come up with rules for your family or a group? What was that like?

SAY: Let's brainstorm some new rules for this group—preferably silly ones. It could be something like "Everyone has to shout his or her name when walking in the door" or "No one is allowed in this room unless he or she is wearing silver pants." The important part is that they should be rules that people outside of the room wouldn't know to follow.

[Have someone write the group's rule ideas on posterboard.]

SAY: Let's vote to choose one rule we will try to follow.

[Have the group vote.]

SAY: It will be kind of easy for us to follow our new rule, because we're all here today and worked together to come up with it. How can we get the rest of the youth who aren't here to follow the rule? What if we wanted our whole congregation to follow the rule—how does

Confirm Teaching Plans

our local church make its rules? [You'll need to find that out at your church if you don't already know!]

- E X P L O R E -

All in the Details 10 minutes

SAY: Trying to trap Jesus with his own words was a pretty common occurrence in the Gospels. Religious leaders and experts were often trying to trick him into saying something that contradicted either his own words or, more important, Scripture. That may have been happening in today's story from the Bible. Will one of you read for us from Mark 12:28-34?

[Ask the volunteer to read the passage.]

SAY: The expert in the Law may have been trying to trick Jesus into holding one part of the Law above the others, or he may honestly have just wondered what Jesus thought. In any case, Jesus comes at it from a different angle.

The first part of his answer, "Israel, listen! Our God is the one Lord, and you must love the Lord your God with all your heart, all your being, with all your mind, and with all your strength," was from a precious Jewish prayer (found in Deuteronomy 6:4-9), one they kept posted on the door frames of their houses. Pious people even wore it strapped on their bodies. Jesus was telling this expert in the law that if he would do that and love his neighbor as he loved himself, he would keep all of the hundreds of laws contained in the Jewish Scripture.

Discussion Questions

• If you were to keep those two commands, which of your house rules would no longer be necessary?

• What keeps us from living out those commandments? Why do we still need other rules to live by?

SAY: The United Methodist Church has gone to great effort to think through and write down what it believes about many social issues. Let's watch a video highlighting a little book called *The Social Principles of The United Methodist Church*. It's made up almost entirely of what the UMC believes the faithful Christian response should be to a wide range of social issues that affect our culture. In a sense, this is our church's answer to the realization that we struggle to always love our neighbor as we love ourselves.

Video Time *5 minutes*

[Show the Lesson 16 video, "A Loving Church."]

ASK: What stood out to you from the video?

- R E F L E C T -

What About . . . ? *5–10 minutes*

SAY: Now turn to your Student Guide and create a response to the question provided.

[Students will make a list of 3 social issues and write a few sentences reflecting on the difference it would make if we applied love to that situation.]

- C R E A T E -

A Church Built on Love
15 minutes

[The students will design a church built on the rule of love. They will use images and words to depict what this church could look like.]

ASK: Who'd be willing to read aloud the instructions for the Create activity in your Student Guide?

[Ask the volunteer to read the instructions in the Student Guide.]

SAY: Take about 10 minutes to complete this activity. Go!

[Allow the students 10 minutes to work on their own.]

SAY: Let's come back together and share our creations.

Discussion Questions *As Time Allows*

• What did you like about this activity? What was challenging?

• What, do you think, distracts us from loving God and others?

- N E X T -

Ideas to Try This Week

[Point out the ideas to try during the week.]

At home: Talk with your family and create a list of all of your family rules. Then assign each rule to one of two categories: love God or love others. Do you have any family rules that don't fit in either category? Do you notice any family rules that are missing?

At school: Jesus tells us to love our neighbor. This week at school love your lunch neighbor. Sit at a table you would typically avoid and get to know someone who is different from you and your friends. What does this experience teach you about yourself? What does it teach you about God?

In your community: Jesus reminds us we love God when we love others. Find an organization in your community that you can volunteer with and help make a positive impact on the world around you (a food pantry, mentoring program, park cleanup, and so forth). How does this act of loving others impact the way you love God?

Lesson

17 So Now What?

LESSON DESCRIPTION: In this lesson, your group will explore what it means to live lives dedicated to mission. We'll use The United Methodist Church's own work in missions as an example of how we can participate individually. Mission doesn't just mean finding stuff to do around your church or community; there are people who dedicate their entire lives to domestic and international mission work.

Lesson Outline		
SECTION	**TOPIC**	**DURATION**
Connect	In Charge	15 minutes
Explore	Getting Started	10 minutes
Reflect	The Work of the Church	5–10 minutes
Create	Snapshots	15 minutes
Next	At home, at school, and in your community	Ideas to try this week

Supply List

Connect: In Charge
❏ Paper
❏ Writing utensils

Explore: Getting Started
❏ Bibles

Reflect: The Work of the Church
❏ Student Guide
❏ Writing utensils

Create: Snapshots
❏ Student Guide
❏ Writing utensils

Next
❏ Student Guides

- C O N N E C T -

In Charge 15 minutes

[**LEADER PREP:** This Connect activity will ask youth to respond as if they are ultimately responsible for responding to situations that generally adults do. The quicker they buy into that, the better this activity will go. Divide your group into at least two groups. Three groups is probably ideal for diversity of opinion without taking too much time, but adjust according to the size of your group. Present the scenarios one at a time and process between.]

SAY: Let's play a game. Imagine that youth are in charge of the world. This was fun at first; and you had a great time driving too fast, staying up too late, and making football a year-round sport. But then you started to notice that other things were happening—things that the adults formerly took care of. You're in charge, though; and you're not ready to give that up yet. So here are a few scenarios that need your attention:

While attending Every Friday Is Lock-In Night (one of your first changes when you came into power), you learn that a videogame console belonging to a youth across town overheated from continuous use and burned down his house. He lost everything but the clothes on his back. His family does not have adequate insurance to rebuild the house. What can our group do to help them?

[Give the groups time to assess. Provide writing materials if they'd prefer to brainstorm on paper.]

Discussion Questions

• So what do we do? Have you encountered a real-life situation anything like this?

• What resources do we lack that would help here? Do we have any way to get those?

SAY: OK, next up: You wake up to thunderstorms and check your weather app, where you find out that a tornado outbreak struck a neighboring state, devastating several small towns. One of them you visited last spring on a mission trip. What can we do to help?

[Group time again. This situation is a little closer to reality, and may have happened nearby or genuinely be within the experience of the group—be sensitive to your context.]

Discussion Questions

• What can we do?

• How do you feel when you hear about real things like this happening to real people? How do you respond?

- E X P L O R E -

Getting Started 10 minutes

SAY: As United Methodists, we're called beyond observing and having opinions on culture to be a missional church. Our Social Principles reveal the voice of the church, but our mission in the world reveals our heart.

How we can help is often the question. We usually want to do more than we can. Sometimes people help in ways that are ultimately unhelpful; it's easy especially in a crisis situation to unintentionally interfere where we intended to help.

The early church faced an unusual situation that called for a quick response. In the story we're about to read, the apostles had carried the news of Jesus to Antioch, where for the first time they started converting Greek-speaking Jews, called Hellenists. The work in Antioch was going so well that Saul and Barnabas ended up staying there for a year. This was actually the first time they were called Christians! While they were there, however, a crisis arose. Let's read the whole story in Acts 11:19-30.

> [Read or have volunteers read aloud the passage from Acts 11:19-30. Then have the students pair up to discuss the following questions.]

• What was the crisis?

• How did the disciples respond?

SAY: It's interesting that the disciples didn't make arrangements to help the new believers in Antioch. Antioch was far north from Judea;

the disciples were essentially sending resources that could have been used in Antioch home to Judea. To their credit, this also meant sending resources away from themselves.

Discussion Questions

• What would you have done, if the youth were in charge of Antioch?

• How could the disciples have overreacted? How could they have done less?

• How, do you think, did they decide what "according to each person's abundance" would amount to (verse 29)?

- REFLECT -

The Work of the Church 5–10 minutes

SAY: Think back to the conversation you just had about the church in Antioch.

ASK: What is one thing you heard your partner say that stood out to you? How would you relate this story and the conversation you had to crises in our world today?

SAY: Write your answers in the speech bubbles in your Student Guide.

- CREATE -

Snapshots 15 minutes

[Students will draw snapshots of the church from the Book of Acts and today living out her mission in the world.]

ASK: Who'd be willing to read aloud the instructions for the Create activity in your Student Guide?

[Ask the volunteer to read the instructions in the Student Guide.]

SAY: Take about 10 minutes to complete this activity. Go!

[Allow the students 10 minutes to work on their own.]

SAY: Let's come back together and share our creations.

Discussion Questions As Time Allows

• What did you like about this activity? What was challenging?

• How, do you think, can the Methodist Church make the biggest difference in the world?

- N E X T -

Ideas to Try This Week

[Point out the ideas to try during the week.]

At home: Go online and visit *umcor.org*. What is one way that your family could partner with the United Methodist Committee on Relief? Share what you learn with your family and start a conversation about ways that you can be a missional community that helps others in the midst of crisis.

At school: In confirmation class, you asked what it would be like if youth were in charge of the world. Talk with your friends at lunch and ask what it would be like if youth were in charge of the school. What would be different? What would stay the same? How would you respond in an emergency or crisis? And most importantly, what would be for lunch each day?

In your community: Talk with your pastor or confirmation leader about things that your church is doing to help the community. Volunteer with a group that already exists or discuss forming a new group. What sort of things would you want to help with? Why?

Unit 4: Our Beliefs

Believing in something is taking a step toward the unknown and having the humility to realize that mystery will always be present. The beauty of our relationship with our Creator is that we don't know everything yet we can trust God, which means taking action on our belief.

What we believe is important—both communally and individually. The United Methodist Church has doctrine that states her institutional beliefs, but she also acknowledges that we are individuals with unique perspectives. Belief is not about being "right" but rather is about providing a structure to create a communal identity and a skeletal framework for individual belief. Identity is important; it helps create parameters for who we are and what we believe. As United Methodists, we have aspects of our belief system that make us unique. How we understand the Bible, how we understand and experience God, and our prayer life are a few examples. This unit will examine some of these beliefs and practices that will help clarify what it means to claim the United Methodist identity.

- CONTENTS -

Lesson

18 Faith and Trust

LESSON DESCRIPTION: This lesson will introduce the idea of trust and how it is essential in the context of our relationship with God. We will focus on the story of Joshua from Scripture, highlighting his trust in God following the passing of his mentor, Moses. We will then use our understanding of trust and the example of Joshua to discover how trust functions in our lives.

Lesson Outline		
SECTION	TOPIC	DURATION
Connect	Trust Icebreaker	10 minutes
	Unit 4 video: "Our Beliefs"	5 minutes
Explore	Scripture on Joshua	15 minutes
Reflect	Sharing Faith Descriptions	10 minutes
Create	Credo	15 minutes
Next	At home, at school, and in your community	Ideas to try this week

Supply List

Connect: Trust Icebreaker
❑ Two trusted, able-bodied adults
❑ Paper
❑ Writing utensils
❑ Unit 4 video: "Our Beliefs"

Explore: Scripture on Joshua
❑ CEB Bibles

Reflect: Sharing Faith Descriptions
❑ Student Guides
❑ Writing utensils

Create: Credo
❑ Student Guides
❑ Magazines
❑ Writing utensils
❑ Scissors
❑ Glue

❑ Writing utensils

Next
❑ Student Guides

Confirm Teaching Plans

- C O N N E C T -

Trust Icebreaker 10 minutes

[*LEADER PREP:* Before class begins, find two able-bodied adults to be on standby to sneak in behind a confirmand volunteer and catch him or her during this next activity.]

SAY: Today we are going to explore faith and trust. What do you think of when you hear the word *faith?*

[Allow for a few responses from the group.]

SAY: Faith is hard to describe, isn't it? For us, it is belief in a being greater than us, a Creator that is not seen or fully understood. Building our faith requires trust. Trust is taking action on our belief.

Now, I need one volunteer from the group to stand up front.

[Ask the volunteer to come forward.]

SAY: I am first going to ask you some questions. But I want you to close your eyes. I promise we will not embarrass you. Do you trust me?

SAY: How is your week going? What was a highlight? What was a challenge from your week? Make sure to keep your eyes shut!

[After the student closes his or her eyes, continue. Signal for the two able-bodied adults to quietly stand behind the volunteer, and keep talking to the volunteer, until they are in position to catch him or her.]

SAY: OK, keep your eyes closed. This next part may seem a little strange. Have you ever heard of a trust fall? Well, I want you to trust me ... even though I am in front of you. Straighten your legs and fall backward without looking ... on the count of three ... 1 ... 2 ... 3!

ASK: Why did you choose for fall back? (*Or Why didn't you fall back?*) Did you sense that someone was behind you?

Discussion Questions

• Would you have fallen backward? Why, or why not?

• Is trust easy or difficult?

• Whom or what do you trust the most?

• What do you trust in that you cannot see?

SAY: We're going to begin this unit with a short video on belief. Trust is a response to beliefs and taking action on our faith. Only when you believe in something or someone can you begin a relationship of trust. As you watch, please write down any questions you have or anything that sticks out to you.

Video Time *5 minutes*

[Show the Unit 4 video: "Our Beliefs."]

ASK: What stood out to you from the video?

- EXPLORE -

Scripture on Joshua *15 minutes*

SAY: Are you ready to listen to a very important and interesting story? Listen carefully to the details so you will be ready to pick up the rest of the story in the Bible.

Most of the Bible (especially the first 39 books) is about a special group of people. They were first called Hebrews, then Israelites, then Jews. They began as a small tribe, then grew into a nation of people.

They were slaves to other nations more than once. A key time in their history is when the leader of the Israelites, Moses, led them out of slavery in Egypt. It was an incredible event where God split a wide sea for them to cross and escape.

Moses is one of the most important people in Jewish and Christian faith because God revealed through him a lot about courage and leadership.

After their escape from Egypt, the Israelites journeyed for years through the harsh desert trying to find their way back home. Before they became slaves, they lhad ived in a beautiful place called the Promised Land. Moses endured years of complaining and struggles leading this group toward home . . . and toward trusting in God.

Along the way, Moses mentored a young man named Joshua. Joshua desired to be like Moses because of how Moses lived out his faith

Confirm Teaching Plans

in God. But after years of leading the people of Israel through the desert, Moses came to a moment in his life where he chose not to trust in God. His punishment was that he would pass away before the people of Israel would return to their Promised Land.

After Moses died, Joshua was put in charge of the nation of Israel. Joshua was scared, as hundreds of thousands of people were now counting on him, and he missed his courageous mentor, Moses.

We are going to pick up the story now as it is found in the Bible. The story is divided in three sections: how God responds to Joshua, how Joshua responds to God, and how God's people respond to Joshua.

> [Ask for three volunteers to read, and hand them Bibles. Have one student read Joshua 1:1-9. Have a second student read Joshua 1:10-15. Have a third read Joshua 1:16-18. Once the entire passage is read, ask the students to read it a second time. Invite others to close their eyes as they listen.]

Discussion Questions

- How does God respond to Joshua? (1:1-9)

- How does Joshua respond to his faith in God? (1:10-15)

- Why, do you think, did others trust Joshua? How did he inspire his people? (1:16-18)

- Can you think of someone in your church like Joshua? Who?

- Is there someone you consider a spiritual mentor because of that person's trust in God?

SAY: Let's think about how trust and faith look in our own lives.

- Who is someone you have followed or that you trust because of his or her faith?

- What, do you think, does it mean to trust God?

- What does trusting God look like in the life of a teenager?

- Does trusting God mean that we never doubt or question God? (How might doubt sometimes be important to faith?)

SAY: This is a really important topic that we could talk about for a long time. You are in a stage of life when questioning and doubting is a natural part of who you are. You are discovering your own independence from your parents and seeking to find what is real and true for you. Part of deepening your faith is asking questions, experiencing doubts, and discovering your own real faith. As strange as it sounds, doubt is a necessary part of faith.

When we talk about trusting God, it really has to do with living in the reality that we are not in control, and resting in the fact that God is. Most of the pain in our lives and in our world is centered in a struggle to find control. Trust is about leaning into the reality that God is only one truly in control (thankfully!).

- R E F L E C T -

Sharing Faith Descriptions *10 minutes*

SAY: Now turn to your Student Guide and journal a response to the questions in the Reflect section:

In your own words, write a one- or two-sentence definition of *faith, trust,* and *belief.* How are they similar? How are they different?

[After 3–4 minutes of reflection, move on to the discussion questions.]

Discussion Questions

• How did you define *faith, trust,* and *belief?*

• How are they similar? How are they different?

• What are some ways we can show our trust in God, living out what we believe?

Confirm Teaching Plans

- C R E A T E -

Credo *15 minutes*

[Each student will write a paragraph or two and draw a picture that captures his or her "credo," what he or she believes. In place of drawing, students may cut images from magazines that depict the credo.]

SAY: Who'd be willing to read aloud the instructions for the Create activity in your Student Guide?

[Ask the volunteer to read the instructions aloud.]

SAY: Take about 10 minutes to complete this activity. Go!

[Allow about 10 minutes for the students to work on their own.]

SAY: Let's come back together and share our creations.

Discussion Questions

As Time Allows

• Who'd be willing to share your credo?

• What did you like about this activity? What was challenging?

• Why, do you think, is belief so hard to define?

- N E X T -

Ideas to Try This Week

[Point out the ideas to try during the week.]

At home: Go online and look up "Our Social Creed" on The United Methodist Church website (*umc.org/what-we-believe/our-social-creed*). Write down a list of words and phrases that you connect with most. Then write down a list of words and phrases that you don't agree with. Show both lists to your pastor or confirmation leader the next time you see them and ask them what they think about "Our Social Creed" and the parts they do and don't connect with.

At school: Talk to a coach or some students who are on a sports team. Ask them how trusting their teammates affects who they are and what they do. Then journal about their responses and your own understanding of trust in God and being a part of a faith community.

In your community: A credo isn't just something you believe with your head. You believe it with your hands and your feet. Take a prayer walk around your block, asking God to lead you to ways that your faith can come to life in the world around you. When you return home write down at least three ideas that you can try.

Confirm Teaching Plans

Lesson

19 Experiencing God

LESSON DESCRIPTION: This lesson will explore four ways to experience God, using the Wesleyan Quadrilateral. We will compare the use of our five senses to help us understand the concept of the Quadrilateral.

Then we will learn more about the four ways of experiencing God, and reflect on how these ways of understanding God look in our lives.

Lesson Outline

SECTION	TOPIC	DURATION
Connect	5 Senses	15 minutes
	Lesson 19 video: "Experiencing God"	5 minutes
Explore	The Wesleyan Quadrilateral	10 minutes
Reflect	Pillars of Your Faith	10 minutes
Create	An Illustrated Quadrilateral	15 minutes
Next	At home, at school, and in your community	Ideas to try this week

Supply List

Connect: 5 Senses
❑ Paper
❑ Writing utensils
❑ Lesson 19 video: "Experiencing God"

Explore: The Wesleyan Quadrilateral
❑ A wind chime with three chimes (inexpensive or homemade)
❑ Electric fan or other source of "wind"
❑ Dry-erase board or flip chart
❑ Student Guides
❑ Sticky notes (8–10 per student)
❑ Writing utensils

Reflect: Pillars of Your Faith
❑ Student Guides
❑ Writing utensils

Create: An Illustrated Quadrilateral
❑ Student Guides
❑ Writing utensils

Next
❑ Student Guides

- CONNECT -

5 Senses *5 minutes*

[Take a minute for the class to get focused. Have the class close their eyes and focus on their breathing. Hand out paper and pens to each person.]

SAY: A lot of what we believe has to do with what we experience. In order to believe in God, we (most often) have to experience God. Psalm 34:8 says, "Taste and see how good the LORD is! The one who takes refuge in him is truly happy!"

As Methodists, we have some distinct ways that we believe we can experience God. Albert Outler, a twentieth-century Methodist scholar, wrote that United Methodists believe in four distinct ways in which we discover God—through Scripture, reason, tradition, and our experiences. We call these four revelations or means to discover God the Wesleyan Quadrilateral. We will come back to this soon.

Video Time *5 minutes*

[Show the Lesson 19 video: "Experiencing God."]

ASK: What stood out to you from the video?

5 Senses (continued) *10 minutes*

Now we are going to try an activity that connects us with our senses. So, relax your shoulders, get comfortable in your seat, and take some deep breaths. For the next few minutes, we will work to remain still and aware of the things we sense around us. This is going to take some focus and patience. Let's begin by closing our eyes.

[Speak slowly and patiently work through this activity. If students get distracted, gently encourage them and bring them back to focus.]

SAY: Focus on your hearing. What do you hear? Your breath? Sounds in the distance? Take 20 seconds and listen quietly and carefully.

[Pause for 20 seconds.]

SAY: Now open your eyes and take a moment to write down what you heard.

Confirm Teaching Plans

Focus on your sense of smell. What does the room smell like? Does it have a distinct smell? Do you smell food? coffee? too much cologne? I know it is hard to not giggle, but take a deep breathe and focus.

[Pause for 20 seconds.]

SAY: Now open your eyes and take a moment to write down what you smelled.

Focus on your sense of taste. What tastes do you have in your mouth? What tastes do you remember from your day? Breathe in with your mouth. Anything new?

[Pause for 20 seconds.]

SAY: Now open your eyes and take a moment to write down what you tasted.

Focus on your sense of touch. What do you feel with your hands? Where are you sitting? How does your chair or the floor feel?

[Pause for 20 seconds.]

SAY: Now open your eyes and take a moment to write down what you felt.

Focus on your sense of sight. What do you see? What do you notice around the room for the first time? What is on the walls? What kind of lighting is there in the room? Who is trying not to laugh?

[Pause for 20 seconds.]

SAY: Now take a moment to write down what you saw.

Gather into groups of 3 or 4 to share your responses. Talk about what was unique to your list and what it had in common with the lists of otehrs in your group.

[After a few minutes of sharing, bring the entire group back together.]

Discussion Questions

• What were the most common things people in your group noticed?

• What were the unique or most interesting things people noticed?

SAY: Senses are a way in which our bodies reveal our surroundings. We use our senses to experience the space and people around us. Our senses are unique, so some people might observe some things while others do not. Our senses can also be communal—we see the same things, we feel the same chairs or floor. Even when we sense the same things, we describe them differently based on who we are and our perceived experience. This is kind of how the Quadrilateral works. Think of the four ways that God reveals Godself to us like they were 4 distinct "spiritual" senses. One way might be more dominant (like our eyesight), but when we use all of our spiritual senses, we can begin to see the picture of God more clearly.

- E X P L O R E -

The Wesleyan Quadrilateral 10 minutes

[**LEADER PREP:** Provide a wind chime with 3 hanging chimes (either inexpensive or homemade will work). Also draw a large Wesleyan Quadrilateral on a dry-erase board or flip chart, with the 4 words as if they were the corners of a square.

Guide the class in the four parts of the Quadrilateral. If you want to read the proper responses in preparation for this lesson, they can be found in paragraph 104 Section 4 in the *Book of Discipline*.]

SAY: When you think of the word *quadrilateral,* you might think of the math term for a figure with four straight sides. That is helpful, but I want to describe the Wesleyan Quadrilateral another way.

I brought in this wind chime. Notice that there are only three chimes. The three chimes represent tradition, reason, and experience. The fourth part is the top from which the chimes hang, and it represents Scripture. Tradition, reason, and experience hang on Scripture, or are filtered through Scripture.

[Use a fan or other means to blow wind through the chimes.]

SAY: The Holy Spirit blows through all of these at different times and together, helping us to sense God. Scripture, tradition, reason, and experience all draw us closer to knowing and being with God. Now, let's take a look at each of these parts of the Quadrilateral.

I need a volunteer to read the short descriptions in the Explore section of the Student Guide for each of the four areas of the Quadrilateral.

Confirm Teaching Plans

[Ask the students to turn to the Explore section in the Student Guide. Ask the volunteer to read the descriptions. Then give each student 8–10 sticky notes.]

SAY: I've created a simple Quadrilateral on the board. For each of the the four areas, I will ask you a question. After I ask the question, I want you to write one or two responses on sticky notes. Are you ready?

[After reading each of the following questions, give students a minute to write responses and place their sticky notes on the board under the corresponding areas.]

ASK:

• How does Scripture connect us with God?

• What are your favorite traditions at church?

• What have you learned through reason that has helped you understand God?

• What experiences have shaped your beliefs about God?

SAY: Looking at this board, you each have examples and thoughts on how God has revealed Godself to you in your life. They are unique and they help define your understanding of God. Seeing how God connects with us in these different ways is evidence that God is present in every corner of our lives.

[Time permitting, have students pick two of their favorite sticky notes that someone else posted, and tell what resonated with them about what was written.]

- R E F L E C T -

Pillars of Your Faith 5 minutes

SAY: Now turn to your Student Guide and follow the directions.

[Allow 5 minutes for the students to work on the Reflect section of the Student Guide.]

- C R E A T E -

An Illustrated Quadrilateral 15 minutes

SAY: Who'd be willing to read aloud the instructions for the Create activity in your Student Guide?

[Ask the volunteer to read the instructions aloud.]

SAY: Take about 10 minutes to complete this activity. Go!

[Allow about 10 minutes for the students to work on their own.]

SAY: Let's come back together and share our creations.

Discussion Questions As Time Allows

• Who'd be willing to share your quadrilaterals?

• What did you like about this activity? What was challenging?

• How, do you think, is the Quadrilateral helpful to us?

- N E X T -

Ideas to Try This Week

[Point out the ideas to try during the week.]

At home: Traditions shape individuals and communities. Talk with your family about the traditions that you share. What traditions mean the most to each person? What impact do they have on the whole family? What traditions do you find confusing? What new traditions would you like to see your family embrace?

At school: Find your science teacher and tell them about "reason" as a part of the Wesleyan Quadrilateral. Talk with them about the ways reason helps us see the world as rich and filled with wonder. How does this conversation connect with your understanding of faith and spirituality?

In your community: Talk with two neighbors about their experience with the church and faith. What can you learn from their experience? What memories from your own life do their experiences bring to the surface?

Confirm Teaching Plans

Lesson 20
The Bible—Not Just a History Book

LESSON DESCRIPTION: This lesson will help students understand where the Bible came from and how it came to be throughout history. Students will begin by sharing their own stories and why those stories are important to them. After understanding their stories, they will move toward understanding where the Bible came from—from it's verbal roots to what we have today.

Lesson Outline		
SECTION	*TOPIC*	*DURATION*
Connect	The Story of Us	15 minutes
Explore	The Bible for Beginners	15 minutes
Reflect	What Do You Say?	10 minutes
Create	Movie Poster	15 minutes
Next	At home, at school, and in your community	Ideas to try this week

Supply List

Connect: The Story of Us
❏ None

Explore: The Bible for Beginners
❏ Copies of the "History of the Bible" handouts
❏ Posterboard
❏ Markers
❏ Writing utensils

Reflect: What Do You Say?
❏ Student Guides
❏ Writing utensils

Create: Movie Poster
❏ Student Guides
❏ Writing utensils

Next
❏ Student Guides

- CONNECT -

The Story of Us 15 minutes

[Ask the students to form groups of 4–5.]

SAY: All right, I want you all to take turns sharing a story from your family. It could be a humorous story; it could be a serious one. It could be something as simple as how your parents met. Your story should include details. Try to be as descriptive as possible. Each person has about 2 minutes to share.

[Allow each student to take a minute or two to share within their group.]

SAY: Has everyone gotten a chance to share something? OK, lets get back together as a class.

ASK: Who'd like to share a story you just heard from someone in your group?

[Allow 2 or 3 students to share.]

ASK: Why are stories so important? Why do you think stories stay with us so easily?

SAY: The stories of our lives are not just a random collection of past experiences. In many ways, our stories define who we are. The stories we choose to tell reveal what kind of people we are and what is important to us. Our beliefs—about ourselves, about the world, and about God—flow out of the stories we take on as our own and share with one another.

The stories in the Bible are also this way. They aren't just a random collection of past experiences. The Bible is a carefully told, curated epic about two special communities' encounters with God. The stories in the Bible reveal deep truths about these two communities—the Israelites and the first Christians—and give us glimpses of what it means to see God up close. The Bible is a story meant to shape who we are and what we believe.

Confirm Teaching Plans

- E X P L O R E -

The Bible for Beginners 15 minutes

SAY: When the Methodist Church merged with the Evangelical United Brethren Church in 1968, not only did we get the cool new title, United Methodist, but we also adopted the Brethren's Confessions of Faith. These confessions are statements that declare what The United Methodist Church believes when it comes to individual aspects of our faith—from who Jesus and the Holy Spirit are to what *good works* and *worship* mean. We will begin our class today by saying together our Confession of Faith on the Bible.

Let's read along together from the Student Guide.

[Ask the students to turn to the "United Methodist Confession of Faith on the Bible" in the Explore section.]

SAY AS A CLASS: We believe the Holy Bible, Old and New Testaments, reveals the Word of God so far as it is necessary for our salvation. It is to be received through the Holy Spirit as the true rule and guide for faith and practice. Whatever is not revealed in or established by the Holy Scriptures is not to be made an article of faith nor is it to be taught as essential to salvation.

[Split the class into 4 equal groups, and provide each group a poster board. Give each student a copy of the "History of the Bible" handout. Assign each group one of the 4 questions: Where did the Bible come from? What is the Torah? What is the New Testament? What is canon? You will be asking them to give a creative answer based on that question.]

SAY: Each group has been assigned one of the four areas on the handout. Below the questions is a summarized answer. You will work together to come up with a creative way to share the answer. You can draw a picture, do a skit, or rewrite the answer in your own words (spoken word).

When time is up, I will have each group come up and share with the rest of the class what they came up with. You may use your phones to research other details about your question not mentioned in the handout.

[Give the groups 10 minutes to prepare a creative answer to their question.]

Lesson 20

- REFLECT -

What Do You Say? 10 minutes

SAY: Based on the four questions we explored about the Bible, we learn that these stories are even older than the written word. Our history of putting the Bible together is as important as the history found in the Scriptures themselves. Their parallels reveal our struggle to better understand God and who we are. When we participate in reading the Scriptures, we invite ourselves into a story that is greater than the words we are reading. We become a part of the story.

Now turn to your Student Guide and journal a response to the questions.

[Allow about 8 minutes for the students to work on their own.]

- CREATE -

Movie Poster 15 minutes

[The students will each design a movie poster that tells people about this ancient and sacred text.]

SAY: Who'd be willing to read aloud the instructions for the Create activity in your Student Guide?

[Ask the volunteer to read the instructions.]

SAY: Take about 10 minutes to complete this activity. Go!

[Allow about 10 minutes for the students to work on their own.]

SAY: Let's come back together and share our creations.

Confirm Teaching Plans

Discussion Questions *As Time Allows*

• Who'd be willing to share your poster?

• What did you like about this activity? What was challenging?

• What did you learn about the Bible today that will stay with you?

- N E X T -

Ideas to Try This Week

[Point out the ideas to try during the week.]

At home: Go online and search for images of old Bibles. What is the oldest one you can find? What is the story behind this ancient book?

At school: Canonization was the process of deciding which books should be in the Bible. How does your school choose which books they will use each year in class? Talk with your teachers, asking them how and why they decided to use the various books you are reading in class.

In your community: Visit 5–7 friends and families from your church, asking them their three favorite books from the Bible. Assemble the results of your community survey and share the results with your pastor or confirmation instructor.

HISTORY OF THE BIBLE

1. Where did the Bible come from?

What we call the Bible began as an oral tradition handed down from generation to generation. These stories were memorized and held as sacred. As communication advanced, the stories were written down and combined into books. These stories detail the experiences of God's people, the Israelites and the early church, and the struggles they had trying to follow God. The Old Testament is filled with celebrations, exile, and even songs that share humanity's ups and downs with God. During Jesus' time, God's people had the Old Testament or the Hebrew Bible. Priests were expected to have the whole of the Scriptures memorized! It was common to quote Scripture, as Jesus does many times in the Gospels.

2. What is the Torah?

The Torah or Pentateuch (five scrolls or books) are the first five books in the Old Testament]. These books are the foundational narrative of the Jewish faith. The stories in the Torah begin with the Creation story and the early beginnings of the Jewish people. It details how they ended up in Egypt and how they were set free. The Torah ends with the death of Moses right before the people of Israel reach the Promised Land. The word *Torah* means "Teachings" or "Guides." Most of what is found in the Books of Leviticus, Numbers, and Deuteronomy are early laws that created the identity of what would be the Jewish nation.

3. What is the New Testament?

The New Testament begins with the four Gospels telling four distinct stories of the life, death, and resurrection of Jesus Christ. It also includes the accounts of the early church and the apostles' ministry in the Book of Acts. The New Testament includes letters written by the apostle Paul and many others and sent to some of the earliest churches. It concludes with the Book of Revelation, a book of apocalyptic literature with the intent of being prophetic.

4. What is canon?

The canon is the collection of books our church fathers and scholars agreed were divinely inspired by God. The canon began about 200 hundred years before Jesus' life, when the Torah was translated into Greek, a common language in the Western world. The New Testament canon was added about 400 years after Jesus' resurrection, at the third Synod or Council of Carthage (A.D. 397) There, 27 books were included to make up the New Testament as we know it today. It wasn't until more than 1,200 years later that the Roman Catholic Church declared this canonization as doctrine at the Council of Trent (A.D. 1545–1563).

Lesson 21
The Bible—A United Methodist View

LESSON DESCRIPTION: This lesson will examine how we, as United Methodists, look at Scripture. We will learn what questions to ask ourselves when reading the Bible in order to better understand its intent and how it is applicable to us today. We will then look at the importance of reading the Bible as a regular Christian practice. This lesson will also provide resources for students to be able to effectively interpret Scripture responsibly.

Lesson Outline		
SECTION	**TOPIC**	**DURATION**
Connect	Out of Context	5 minutes
Explore	Context! Context! Context!	20 minutes
Reflect	What Is It to You?	10 minutes
Create	Bible Blackout	15 minutes
Next	At home, at school, and in your community	Ideas to try this week

Supply List

Connect: Out of Context
❑ CEB Bible

Explore: Context! Context! Context!
❑ Posterboard or dry-erase board
❑ Markers
❑ Writing utensils
❑ Student Guides
❑ Sticky notes (3–4 per student)

Reflect: What Is It to You?
❑ Student Guides
❑ Writing utensils

Create: Bible Blackout
❑ Student Guides
❑ Permanent markers

Next
❑ Student Guides

- C O N N E C T -

Out of Context *5 minutes*

SAY: I am going to read a few quotations, and I want you to help us by telling what you think the quotation means.

SAY: "Money is the root of all evil." Who has heard this before? What do you think this means?

[Allow a few students to answer.]

SAY: Do any of you know where this quotation comes from? Someone pull out their CEB Bible and read 1 Timothy 6:10 for us.

[Ask a volunteer to read the passage aloud: "The *love* of money is the root of all kinds of evil" (1 Timothy 6:10, italics added).]

SAY: This is where we get this infamous quotation. After reading this directly from the Bible, do we have a different meaning?

[Allow a student or two to answer.]

SAY: Have you heard of the quotation "Nice guys finish last"? This one's pretty self-explanatory, right?

ASK: Do any of you know where this quotation comes from?

[Allow a student or two to answer.]

SAY: It comes from a field manager for the Brooklyn Dodgers, Leo Durocher, when he was talking about how Giants right fielder Mel Ott was too nice, implying that was the reason they didn't win. Do you know what place the Giants came in that particular year? Seventh. When this quotation was reprinted in *Baseball Digest,* it was changed from "Nice guys finish seventh" to "Nice guys finish last." History suggests that the original quotation doesn't mean what we use it to mean today.

ASK: All right, who has heard of two people being called "star-crossed lovers"? Do any of you know where this came from?

[Allow students to answer that it came from Shakespeare's *Romeo and Juliet.*]

ASK: Do any of you know what it means to be star-crossed lovers?

SAY: When we think of star-crossed lovers, we think of two people who were brought together by fate. But when William Shakespeare labeled his two main characters as "star-crossed," he actually meant that they were destined to die because the stars or fate had crossed them. Shakespeare is reminding the reader that his story is a tragedy. I hope you'll think twice about using this phrase loosely.

Now I'm going to say a quotation, and you'll tell me who said it. Ready?

"Luke, I am your father."

[Allow the class to shout Darth Vader.]

SAY: Actually, Vader did not say this. He said, "No, I am your father." Although it seems the same, the actual words imply that Vader is arguing about who Luke claims to be his father rather than just telling him. It's a small change, but sometimes that makes all the difference.

ASK: Have you ever been taken out of context? I mean, have you ever said something and someone else claimed that you stated something that was different than your original intent?

[Have a student or two share if they are willing.]

SAY: When we look at quotations at the surface, sometimes we get completely different meanings than the writers' original intentions. But after some research, we learn that money isn't evil—just the love of it; we learn that "star-crossed" is not a term of endearment, and we learn that Luke thought that someone else was his father before the truth was revealed.

We need to look at the Bible in this way as well. Sometimes finding the meaning of a piece of Scripture means looking at the whole story and researching its history.

- EXPLORE -

Context! Context! Context! 20 minutes

[**LEADER PREP:** Divide a large posterboard or dry-erase board into three equal sections by drawing lines. At the top of the first section, write: "The Scriptures are received through the Holy

Spirit." At the top of the middle section, write: "as the true rule and guide for faith and practice." At the top of the third section, write: "Interpret Responsibly."

Hand out writing utensils and 3–4 sticky notes to each person.]

SAY: Our Confession of Faith says: the Scriptures are "received through the Holy Spirit as the true rule and guide for faith and practice."

As Methodists, we believe that the Bible is a guide through faith and life; but we also understand that Scripture needs to be interpreted responsibly in order for us to understand its intent.

[Point to the words on the first section of the board.]

SAY: The first part of the statement says the Scriptures are 'received through the Holy Spirit." Let's read a verse that relates to this truth. Who'd be willing to read John 14:26 aloud?

[Ask a student volunteer to read this verse: "The Companion, the Holy Spirit, whom the Father will send in my name, will teach you everything and will remind you of everything I told you" (John 14:26).]

SAY: Jesus said in this verse that God's Spirit would come to teach and guide his followers. Pretty cool.

So, here is the first question I want you to write a response to on a sticky note:

ASK: How, do you think, does God help us understand Scripture?

[Repeat the question.]

SAY: Take a moment to write on a sticky note what this means to you.

[After the students write, ask them to share what they have written and to place their sticky notes on the board.]

SAY: This is a hard thing to describe. We are talking about something in the spiritual realm. God gives us new understanding and eyes to see the Bible through the Spirit working in us.

SAY: Now, let's look at the second question.

ASK: How, do you think, is the Bible a "rule and guide for faith and practice"?

Confirm Teaching Plans

SAY: Take a moment to write on a sticky note what this means to you.

[After the students write, ask them to share what they have written and to place their sticky notes on the board.]

SAY: The Bible helps us understand what faith is. When our faith is challenged or even celebrated, the stories we find about our ancestors help us know that we are not alone.

Let's continue with the third question.

ASK: What, do you think, does it mean to "interpret the Bible responsibly"?

SAY: Take a moment to write on a sticky note what this means to you.

[After the students write, ask them to share what they have written and to place their sticky notes on the board.]

SAY: We are going to dig deeper into this last part now. Who'd be willing to read Jeremiah 29:11 for us?

[Ask a student volunteer to read this verse: "I know the plans I have in mind for you, declares the LORD; they are plans for peace, not disaster, to give you a future filled with hope" (Jeremiah 29:11).]

SAY: When we read the Bible, often our first thought is "What does this mean for me?" This is an important question, but it shouldn't be the first question we ask. When interpreting Scripture, we should first ask, "What does it mean to the people it was originally written to?" This is called "seeking context." We need to dig to find out what was going on in the time and place in which that Scripture was written.

Reading Scripture is kind of like starting to watch a movie in the middle. It takes us some time and effort to find out what is going on in the story to accurately interpret it. Let's reread this verse to illustrate what I mean.

ASK: Who'd be willing to read Jeremiah 29:11 for us again?

[Ask a student volunteer to reread the verse.]

SAY: When we understand the bigger story surrounding this verse, we discover that God is speaking through a prophet—a human messenger named Jeremiah—encouraging an ancient group of people—the people of Israel—who were in slavery and exiled to Babylon. This wasn't the first time that the people of Israel had been enslaved; this kept happening to them. They were looking for a message of hope from God in the midst of their suffering.

ASK: What are some ways we can find out more of context (the bigger story) of a verse like this?

SAY: One of the simplest ways to find out context is to read the book that surrounds the verse. More than 70 percent of Scripture is narrative, meaning that it is a part of a story. So if we take time to read around a verse or a chapter, we can learn a lot.

Another way to learn about context to help us understand Scripture is through external resources, such as pastors, books and commentaries, and Bible notes.

We can also discover context and meaning by studying the language. The Bible was originally written in the ancient languages of Hebrew, Aramaic, and Greek. Here's what I mean:

Let's hear Jeremiah 29:11 again.

> [Ask a student volunteer to read the verse a third.]

SAY: In the original Hebrew language the word used for "plans" is *machasabah* (MAK-ush-ah-bah) which is better translated as "thoughts." So it may be better to read this Scripture as "I know the thoughts I have in mind for you."

The Hebrew word for "peace" used in this verse is *shalom,* which better translates as "completeness" or "wholeness."

> [Have a student volunteer read aloud the quotation from Archbishop Desmond Tutu, which can be found on page 84 of the Student Guide.]

SAY: By exploring the original languages, we see more dimensions to the Scripture. In a verse like Jeremiah 29:11, new meanings open up to us as we uncover God's thoughts and wishes for a future filled with hope and wholeness for the people of Israel.

Discussion Questions

• How does knowing the background and context change the way you look at this verse?

• How, do you think, did hearing this verse make the people of Israel feel?

- How, do you think, did God want to bring the enslaved Israelites hope and completeness (shalom)?

SAY: Now you may be wondering, "If Scripture was written to someone else (to an ancient community), what does it have to do with us (or me)?" That is a great question. The simplest way I can explain this is that even though Scripture was not written (directly) *to* us, it was written *for* us.

That means that God reveals meaning for our lives out of the ancient stories in the Bible. This is called "application."

Let's hear Jeremiah 29:11 a final time.

[Have a student read the verse again]

Discussion Questions

- If God desired completeness for the Israelites in slavery, what might that mean for us? for you?

- What encouragement or challenge does this verse have for us?

SAY: When reading the Bible, we need to look at it through the lens of humility. When reading, we need to know who is writing the Scripture, to whom the Scripture is being written, and what is going on during the time the Scripture is written. When we can make these connections, then we no longer take the Scripture at face value but rather learn to read beyond the words. Having one foot in the times of the Scripture and one foot in the present allows us to begin to understand what was the intent of the written word and how it could apply to us thousands of years later.

- R E F L E C T -

What Is It to You? 10 minutes

SAY: Now turn to your Student Guide and journal a response to the questions in the Reflect section.

[Allow about 10 minutes for the students to work on their own.]

- C R E A T E -

Bible Blackout *15 minutes*

SAY: Who'd be willing to read aloud the instructions for the Create activity in your Student Guide?

[Ask the volunteer to read the instructions.]

SAY: Take about 10 minutes to complete this activity. Go!

[Allow about 10 minutes for the students to work on their own.]

SAY: Let's come back together and share our creations.

Discussion Questions *As Time Allows*

• Who'd be willing to share your Bible Blackout?

• What did you like about this activity? What was challenging?

• Why, do you think, is it important to understand the context and bigger story when reading the Bible?

• How will today's lesson help you to better connect with the Bible?

- N E X T -

Ideas to Try This Week

[Point out the ideas to try during the week.]

At home: Read the Bible every day. Search online for "this week's lectionary text," click the link at the top of the page, and find the texts for this coming Sunday. Choose one to read each day this week. Journal your thoughts and reflections after you read each one.

At school: Bring your Bible to school with you. Read it when you have free moments. Pay attention to how carrying this book sparks different conversations with your friends and classmates.

In your community: One thing that makes the Bible unique is the way it feels different when read in different environments. Take your Bible and go on an adventure, reading the same passage (Psalm 46) in various locations. Find a quiet place under a tree. Stand next to a busy street. Sit in a space crowded with people. Find the tallest building you can access. How do these different environments impact the way you read the Bible?

Lesson

22 The Holy Trinity

LESSON DESCRIPTION: This lesson will examine the Holy Trinity and how it helps us understand God. This lesson will help students articulate the trinitarian theology with the understanding that it is still a belief that remains difficult to pin down.

Lesson Outline

SECTION	TOPIC	DURATION
Connect	Who Are We?	10 minutes
Explore	Trinitarian Visual	10 minutes
Reflect	Understanding God	15 minutes
Create	Three Logos in One	15 minutes
Next	At home, at school, and in your community	Ideas to try this week

Supply List

Connect: Who Are We?
❑ Posterboard or dry-erase board
❑ Marker
❑ Writing utensils
❑ Half-sheets of paper

Explore: Trinitarian Visual
❑ Three pieces of rope (each at least a foot long)
❑ CEB Bibles

Reflect: Understanding God
❑ Student Guides
❑ Writing utensils

Create: Three Logos in One
❑ Paper
❑ Student Guides
❑ Writing utensils

Next
❑ Student Guides

- C O N N E C T -

Who Are We? *10 minutes*

[*LEADER PREP:* Have a piece of posterboard (or a dry-erase board) set up with the words "Who Are We?" written at the top. Also have half-sheets of paper ready to hand out to each student.]

SAY: Who are you? If someone were to come up to you and ask you this, what would you say? Now, I don't want to know what you *do*. For instance, if you are an athlete or a gamer or a cheerleader, that shouldn't define who you are.

[Hand out a half-sheet of paper to each student.]

SAY: I want you to take a few minutes to think about this. Who are you? How would you define yourself? Who are you on the inside? Write your answer on the paper.

[To help the conversation, the leader could give ideas such as *brother, daughter, child, human, loved*.]

SAY: All right, everyone, I know that this was probably difficult to think about since we are so used to defining ourselves based on what we do; but I really want to stretch your minds a bit today. Give me some of the ideas you wrote down, and I will write them on our board.

ASK: Why, do you think, is it hard to define who you are with words?

[Allow several students to answer.]

SAY: We all have different things that make us who we are. To some, we are simply an acquaintance; to some, we are a friend; and to some, we are a loved one—sister, brother, spouse. We are loved, liked, disliked, human, boy, girl, and so forth. And while one person might label us as one thing, another might label us as another. They are not just pieces of a puzzle that make up you but rather ideas that describe all of you from different people, based on their experiences of you.

Now, flip the paper over, and quickly write words that describe who God is. Not what God does, but who God is. Write the first things that come to your mind. I am going to give you about 30 seconds.

[Allow 30 seconds for the students to write their answers.]

ASK: What did you write down? I will write them on our board.

[Ask the students to volunteer their answers, and write the answers on the board.]

ASK: Why do you think it is hard to define who God is with words?

[Allow several students to answer.]

- EXPLORE -

Trinitarian Visual *10 minutes*

[Hold up three pieces of rope.]

SAY: I need a volunteer to come up and hold these pieces of rope.

[Have the volunteer hold up all three pieces of rope together.]

SAY: Right now, you see three distinct pieces of rope, right?

[Start braiding the three rope pieces together.]

SAY: Now, even though there are three pieces of rope, made of the same substance, now we have one braid. When we combine these three pieces, we make one thing. There are not three braids but one. Although we cannot create a visual that perfectly represents the mystery of the Holy Trinity, this can help us begin to understand the distinctness and unity of the Father, Son, and Holy Spirit.

All right, everyone, lets crack open our Bibles. Who will read Matthew 28:19 aloud for us?

[Ask a student volunteer to read: "Therefore, go and make disciples of all nations, baptizing them in the name of the Father and of the Son and of the Holy Spirit" (Matthew 28:19).]

SAY: You might recognize this passage. It is often called the Great Commission. Jesus says this to his disciples after his resurrection. In Matthew, this scene concludes his account of Jesus; so for Matthew, it is important for the story to end in our hands. Jesus calls his eleven and tells them to go and change the world, to teach what they have witnessed and what they have been taught.

ASK: What does Jesus ask them to do?

[Allow a student to answer.]

SAY: Jesus tells them to make disciples, signified by baptizing people in the name of the Father, Son, and Holy Spirit. The three persons *are* God. We describe this as the Trinity. Stay with me as we look at another piece of Scripture. Who of you will read Genesis 1:26 aloud for us?

[Ask a student volunteer to read: "Then God said, 'Let us make humanity in our image to resemble us so that they may take charge of the fish of the sea, the birds of the sky, the livestock, all the earth, and all the crawling things on earth'" (Genesis 1:26).]

Discussion Question

• Did you notice anything about how God describes Godself in this passage?

SAY: When God speaks of Godself in this verse, God uses the plural pronoun "us." (*If no one answers this, then share with the class.*) Isn't it interesting that we can go all the way back to the beginning of the Bible and find God in the middle of creating everything describes God's self in the plural?

OK, one more Scripture for us to read. Who of you will read John 10:30-36 for us?

[Ask a student volunteer to read John 10:30-36 aloud.]

SAY: Here Jesus is responding to local leaders questioning his authority. Jesus is celebrating the Festival of Dedication, or Hanukkah, and some who oppose Jesus ask him to tell them that he is the Christ. Jesus masterfully responds by saying "I and the Father are one" (verse 30).

In The United Methodist Church, we have adopted what we call the Articles of Religion, statements that declare what we believe. Let me read the Article on The Holy Trinity. Think about what stands out to you when I read this.

[Read the statement below, from the United Methodist Articles of Religion on the Holy Trinity (*http://www.umc.org/what-we-believe/ the-articles-of-religion-of-the-methodist-church*), Article I—Of Faith in the Holy Trinity.]

READ: "There is but one living and true God, everlasting, without body or parts, of infinite power, wisdom, and goodness; the maker and preserver of all things, both visible and invisible. And in unity of this Godhead there are three persons, of one substance, power, and eternity—the Father, the Son, and the Holy Ghost."

ASK: What stood out to you from this article? Any new insights?

SAY: When it comes to the Trinity, some focus on the three persons and others focus on the oneness of God.

Theologically, we can focus on both. The Trinity implies three persons; but Christianity remains monotheistic (we believe in one God), so we need to understand the oneness as well.

- R E F L E C T -

Understanding God 15 minutes

SAY: Our founder, John Wesley, believed that seeing God as three-in-one is an essential way of understanding who God is. This way of understanding God—called trinitarian theology—is an important and central part of Christian doctrine. It has been a part of our theological tradition since the Nicene and Apostles' Creeds and before.

Now turn to your Student Guide and journal a response to the Reflect section.

[Allow about 10 minutes for the students to work on their own.]

- C R E A T E -

Three Logos in One 15 minutes

SAY: Who'd be willing to read the instructions aloud for the Create activity in your Student Guide?

[Ask the volunteer to read the instructions.]

SAY: Take about 10 minutes to complete this activity. Go!

[Allow about 10 minutes for the students to work on their own.]

SAY: Let's come back together and share our creations.

Lesson 23
Who Is God? (And Who God Isn't)

LESSON DESCRIPTION: This lesson will examine the many specific ways in which we use to perceive God. It will help us challenge ourselves to think about God in both the abstract and the relationship sense. We'll explore the story of Job as a backdrop to how we perceive God..

Lesson Outline		
SECTION	**TOPIC**	**DURATION**
Connect	God as ...	20 minutes
Explore	Lesson 23 video: "Who Is God? (And Who God Isn't)"	5 minutes
	Scripture on Job	10 minutes
Reflect	Reflections of Job	5 minutes
Create	Job's Prayer Journal	15 minutes
Next	At home, at school, and in your community	Ideas to try this week

Supply List

Connect: God as ...
❑ Drawing paper
❑ Student Guide

Explore: Scripture on Job
❑ CEB Bible
❑ Lesson 23 video: "Who Is God? (And Who God Isn't)"

Reflect: Reflections of Job
❑ Student Guides
❑ Writing utensils

Create: Job's Prayer Journal
❑ Student Guides
❑ Writing utensils

Next
❑ Student Guides

Confirm Teaching Plans

- C O N N E C T -

God as . . . *20 minutes*

[Together, your class will examine different ways in which we perceive God. After each perception is revealed, students will depict their perception and share it with the class.]

SAY: We all have perceptions of God. How we perceive God determines how we consciously and subconsciously include (or don't include) God in our daily lives. We probably don't see God one particular way. Sometimes our feelings about God change based on where we are and what is going on in our lives. Keep in mind that our perception of God does not define God. God remains constant and present in our lives always.

Fold a piece of paper in half so that you have two equal rectangular sections. Then unfold the paper. Then fold it in half the other way so that you have four equal sections. In each of these four boxes, you will sketch and write what you think of a common perception of God.

1. The first common perception is "God as the Great Oz." Write "God as the Great Oz" in one of your boxes. Be sure to leave room to draw.

In the book and movie *The Wizard of Oz,* the people of Oz see their leader as a great and powerful being confined in a castle. In the story, Dorothy and her friends have to make a journey to find the mysterious Wizard. He is distant and unapproachable, too busy to be bothered with the troubles of everyday life. Sometimes we think of God like this—as a distant being sitting in the clouds, unapproachable and mysterious, removed from our day-to-day realities.

In the box on your paper, take a minute to draw to write what God acts like as the Great Oz.

[Give students a couple minutes to draw God as the Great Oz.]

ASK: Who would like to share your drawing or thoughts about this?

[Allow several students to share.]

ASK: What is limited or wrong with this perception of God? How is God more than this?

[Allow several students to answer.]

SAY: God is all around us. God is not in a distant place, separate. God is living within our lives daily. We don't have to journey to find God, we just need to be present and attuned to God's presence all around us and in us.

2. The second common perception is "God as the Big Vending Machine." Now write "God as the Big Vending Machine" in one the boxes on your paper. Leave space to draw in.

SAY: Sometimes people go to God only for a quick fix: Insert the right prayer; select what you want; and then God drops your wishes from the sky, meeting all of your desires. We can just get whatever we want, and God is there to deliver. Now draw God as the Big Vending Machine.

[Give students a couple minutes to draw God as the Big Vending Machine.]

ASK: Who would like to share your drawing or thoughts about this?

[Allow several students to share.]

ASK: What is limited or wrong with this perception of God? How is God more than this?

[Allow several students to answer.]

SAY: God isn't whatever we want God to be. God doesn't just exist for us and our purposes; we exist for God's purposes. When we align with God's purposes in the world, that is when we find meaning and fulfillment in life.

3. The third common perception of God is "God as Giant Judge." Write "God as Giant Judge" in one the boxes on your paper. Again, leave space to draw in.

SAY: Sometimes we think of God as a big eye in the sky who watches us, waiting in anticipation for us to make mistakes and to pass judgment. Now draw God as the Giant Judge.

[Give the students a couple minutes to draw God as Giant Judge.]

ASK: Who would like to share your drawing or thoughts about this?

[Allow several students to share.]

ASK: What is limited or wrong with this perception of God? How is God more than this?

[Allow several students to answer.]

SAY: God is not waiting to pass judgment on us for our mistakes. God is present at times of mourning and at times of celebration. (See Ecclesiastes!) God resides in our laughter and our tears.

4. The fourth common perception of God is "God as Cosmic Life Coach." Write "God as Cosmic Life Coach" in the last box on your paper, leaving space to draw in.

A trend today for rich and famous people is to have a life coach, someone to help them with self-improvement and to continue to actualize their dreams of success. What they are seeking is a life of happiness and fulfillment, free from pain. Sometimes we think that God is our personal life coach, existing to pave a path of happiness and prosperity especially for us, removing pain and discomfort from our lives. Now draw God as the Cosmic Life Coach.

[Give the students a couple minutes to draw God as Cosmic Life Coach.]

ASK: Who would like to share your drawing or thoughts about this?

[Allow several students to share.]

ASK: What is limited or wrong with this perception of God? How is God more than this?

[Allow several students to answer.]

SAY: God does want to bring meaning and fulfillment in our lives, but makes no promise about removing pain and suffering. God does care deeply for each of us, but God seems to have greater purposes than to exist for our own comfort.

We cannot make God out to be what we want God to be. When we can except who God is, then we can being to transform ourselves. When we are transformed, only then can we witness God in our lives all the time and in everything. We cannot describe God based on who we are but rather we need to describe ourselves based on who God is. We need to break down the walls of perception to get a clearer idea of who God is. Only then can we be transformed and allow God to live in our lives the way God intends.

- E X P L O R E -

Video Time 5 minutes

[Show the Lesson 23 video: "Who Is God? (And Who God Isn't)."]

ASK: What stood out to you from the video?

Scripture on Job *10 minutes*

SAY: The story of Job is about a man who loses everything. Job began as a wealthy man with a great big family; but toward the end of the story, we find him with nothing—no job, no wealth, and no family. Right before the thirty-eighth chapter, Job begins to question where God is (Job 37:23-24) In the chapter 38, we hear God's response.

SAY: Close your eyes as I read you some Scripture.

[Ask the students to close their eyes as you read Job 37:23-24 and 38:1-38 aloud.]

SAY: Think about a time when you were upset and you asked God where God was in the mess.

[Pause for 20 seconds.]

SAY: Keep that thought in your minds as we hear this Scripture again.

[As they hear the Scripture the second time, have the students pretend that God is responding to their request.]

Discussion Question

• What do you think of God's response to Job?

- R E F L E C T -

Reflections of Job *5 minutes*

SAY: Sometimes it's difficult to see God at certain times in our lives. But because we believe in a God who invests in our lives, we can have faith that God is present. We might not see it in the present, but, if we look back, we can see how masterfully God works in all things.

ASK: Who'd be willing to read aloud Job 42:1-6 for us?

[Ask the volunteer to read the Scripture.]

SAY: Now turn to your Student Guide and journal your response in the Reflect section.

- CREATE -

Job's Prayer Journal 15 minutes

SAY: Who'd be willing to read aloud the instructions for the Create activity in your Student Guide?

[Ask the volunteer to read the instructions.]

SAY: Take about 10 minutes to complete this activity. Go!

[Allow about 10 minutes for the students to work on their own.]

SAY: Let's come back together and share our creations.

Discussion Questions As Time Allows

• Who'd be willing to share your prayer journal for Job?

• What did you like about this activity? What was challenging?

• What stands out to you about God's interaction with Job?

- NEXT -

Ideas to Try This Week

[Point out the ideas to try during the week.]

At home: Read the entire Book of Job. If possible, read it in a single sitting. Then go online and search for "the story of Job" to find out more about this ancient story. Spend some time journaling to reflect on what this story teaches you about God.

At school: Job's friends show up and fail to provide the comfort that he truly needs. Who do you know at school who is in need of comfort? What can you do to support them? Where is God in the midst of whatever they are going through?

In your community: Read Job 38. Then take a walk around your neighborhood with your eyes open to see God in the wonder of the created world. When you return home write your own version of Job 38 based on the things you saw on your walk.

- C R E A T E -

Job's Prayer Journal *15 minutes*

SAY: Who'd be willing to read aloud the instructions for the Create activity in your Student Guide?

[Ask the volunteer to read the instructions.]

SAY: Take about 10 minutes to complete this activity. Go!

[Allow about 10 minutes for the students to work on their own.]

SAY: Let's come back together and share our creations.

Discussion Questions *As Time Allows*

• Who'd be willing to share your prayer journal for Job?

• What did you like about this activity? What was challenging?

• What stands out to you about God's interaction with Job?

- N E X T -

Ideas to Try This Week

[Point out the ideas to try during the week.]

At home: Read the entire Book of Job. If possible, read it in a single sitting. Then go online and search for "the story of Job" to find out more about this ancient story. Spend some time journaling to reflect on what this story teaches you about God.

At school: Job's friends show up and fail to provide the comfort that he truly needs. Who do you know at school who is in need of comfort? What can you do to support them? Where is God in the midst of whatever they are going through?

In your community: Read Job 38. Then take a walk around your neighborhood with your eyes open to see God in the wonder of the created world. When you return home write your own version of Job 38 based on the things you saw on your walk.

Lesson
24 Prayer: Talking With God

LESSON DESCRIPTION: This lesson will help students begin to understand what prayer is and how to practice it on a regular basis. We will also look at the Lord's Prayer as an example of how to pray.

Lesson Outline

SECTION	TOPIC	DURATION
Connect	Letter to God	10 minutes
Explore	Prayer Outline	15 minutes
Reflect	Unfamiliar Versions	10 minutes
Create	In My Own Words	15 minutes
Next	At home, at school, and in your community	Ideas to try this week

Supply List

Connect: Letter to God
❑ Paper
❑ Writing utensils

Explore: Prayer Outline
❑ Posterboard
❑ Marker
❑ Sticky notes
❑ Student Guides

Reflect: Unfamiliar Versions
❑ Student Guides
❑ Writing utensils

Create: In My Own Words
❑ Student Guides
❑ Writing utensils

Next
❑ Student Guides

Confirm Teaching Plans

- C O N N E C T -

Letter to God *10 minutes*

SAY: When your pray, what do you say? Has anyone ever asked you to pray? How did you respond?

Now turn to a partner and say a quick prayer for that person. Don't overthink this. Just ask your partner for one area you can pray about for him or her.

[Give students 3–4 minutes to do this. Hand out pens and paper to each student.]

SAY: I have given each of you some paper to write a letter. Before Twitter and Facebook—and even phones—the best way to contact people who lived long distances away was to take a piece of paper and write down thoughts and updates about our lives.

I want you to write a letter to God. Let God know your thoughts, and give God updates about what is going on in your life. This is something just for you. You will not be sharing this with the class.

[Give students 7–8 minutes to do this.]

Discussion Questions

• What was this experience like?

• Is it easier for you to write a prayer or speak it? Why do you think that is?

SAY: We sometimes think of prayer as the formal exercise in which we ask things of God and perhaps give thanks, but do we share who we are with God? Some of you might be thinking, "God already knows everything about me and my life." and you would be right, but God still wants you to share because sharing is a sign of intimacy.

- E X P L O R E -

Prayer Outline *15 minutes*

[**LEADER PREP:** Make a posterboard for each of the letters of the word *ACTS*. Then write what each letter means under each letter.

As you introduce each phrase, you will hang up the posterboards in the room. The students will need these for the Reflect and Create activities.]

SAY: There isn't just one way to pray. Sometimes just saying thanks can be enough. Last week we discussed different assumptions about God. Prayer coincides with these. God doesn't want us to pray only when we need something. God doesn't want us to pray only when things are tough or when things seem great. God wants us to pray all the time . . . like breathing. Prayer is simply communication with God.

There are many different types of prayers. There are communal prayers. Examples of these would be the Great Thanksgiving which we find in the sacrament of Communion. Opening and closing prayers in worship are also communal prayers. Invocations that we hear at social events are a form of prayer. Even the silly songs we sometimes sing before a meal are prayers!

[Hand out a few sticky notes to each student.]

SAY: OK, some of us have different prayers we have grown up with. Take a sticky note or two to name some of these prayers you know. The prayers could be something that we say on Sunday mornings or a family prayer you have learned. When you are finished, take your sticky notes and place them in the front of the class.

[After everyone is finished, take a few minutes to share what students have written. Note: John Wesley used to wake up early in the morning to pray for about 4 hours even before he started his day!]

SAY: Praying takes practice, just like being good at conversations requires practice. Remember that conversations have two parts: speaking and listening. Sometimes prayers can be simply being quiet and listening. Methodists love acronyms. Remember the acronym *ACTS* when thinking about prayer. These are listed your Student Guide.

Adoration: Give God praise and honor.

Confession: Tell God what is heavy on your heart.

Thanksgiving: Let God know what you're grateful for.

Supplication: Pray for the needs of others.

SAY: Let's look at each of these in more detail.

First is adoration, or giving praise. I want you to take a moment and think of one or two words that give honor to God. Raise your hand when you have one.

[Allow 2 or 3 students to give examples.]

SAY: The second part is the confession. This is probably the hardest one because this is when we let God know the burdens on our hearts. Now close your eyes. With your eyes closed, I want you to hold your fists tightly. Think of the stress you have created through bad decisions you have made. What are things you are not proud of? You might be upset with someone, you might have hurt someone, or you might just be angry about something. Do you have something on your mind yet?

Now, silently share this with God. And as you do, release your tightened fists and have your palms facing upward. As you feel your hands relaxing, think of this action as releasing what is on your heart and giving it to God. Amen.

Now keep your eyes closed. Think of something that you are truly thankful for. This could be your parents, your friends, your awesome confirmation class. When you have something, open your eyes, come up, and write on a sticky note what it is that you are thankful for. When you are finished, place the sticky note on the board next to the word *Thanksgiving*.

[Allow the students to place their sticky notes.]

SAY: The final part of prayer is supplication, or praying for others. I want you to pair up and find a space in the room with your partner. Share one thing that you need prayer for, then pray for each other.

[Allow a couple of minutes for the partners to pray for each other.]

SAY: There really is no wrong way to pray. God wants to hear from us regardless of what we say. God desires our attention, and prayer is a spiritual practice that can deepen our relationship with God.

- REFLECT -

Unfamiliar Versions 10 minutes

SAY: Now turn to your Student Guide and take 10 minutes to journal your own ACTS prayer.

[Allow the students 10 minutes to complete their prayers.]

- CREATE -

In My Own Words 15 minutes

SAY: Who'd be willing to read the instructions aloud for the Create activity in your Student Guide?

[Ask the volunteer to read the instructions.]

SAY: Take about 10 minutes to complete this activity. Go!

[Allow about 10 minutes for the students to work on their own.]

SAY: Let's come back together and share our creations.

Discussion Questions As Time Allows

• Who'd be willing to share your ACTS prayer?

• What did you like about this activity? What was challenging?

• How might our lesson today inspire you to pray?

- NEXT -

Ideas to Try This Week

[Point out the ideas to try during the week.]

At home: Each night this week before you go to bed, write down a prayer using the ACTS prayer structure. Then pray that prayer again when you wake up the next morning.

At school: Be extra observant this week at school. What do you notice happening around you? How can you pray for your friends, your classmates, and your teachers? Write down the names of the people you are praying for this week.

In your community: Find a local newspaper or local news website. Read about the things happening in your community. Say a prayer for each one.

Lesson
25 Prayer: Listening to God

LESSON DESCRIPTION: This lesson will encourage students to be still and know God. Sometimes prayer isn't about saying the right thing, but rather it is about taking the time to push everything aside for focus on God.

Lesson Outline		
SECTION	**TOPIC**	**DURATION**
Connect	Interrupting Partner	15 minutes
Explore	Scripture on Elijah	10 minutes
Reflect	Meditating on God	10 minutes
Create	The Sound of Silence	15 minutes
Next	At home, at school, and in your community	Ideas to try this week

Supply List

Connect: Interrupting Partner
❏ None

Explore: Scripture on Elijah
❏ CEB Bibles
❏ Writing utensils

Reflect: Meditating on God
❏ Student Guides
❏ Writing utensils

Create: The Sound of Silence
❏ Student Guides
❏ Writing utensils

Next
❏ Student Guides

- C O N N E C T -

Interrupting Partner *15 minutes*

SAY: All right, everyone please pair up. When you have a partner, let me know by raising your hands.

[Let everyone find partner.]

SAY: OK, I need for one partner to go wait in the hall.

[Wait until half of the group is in the hall, out of earshot.]

SAY: In a moment, I am going to ask your partners to come back into the room. I will ask them to share with you their favorite movie and to tell you why.

When your partner begins to share, ignore him or her. Make it obvious that you aren't paying attention. You might start talking about something else, start talking to someone else, even walk away for a second.

[Invite the hallway group to come back into the room.]

SAY: Group that was in the hallway, you have 2 minutes to share with your partner your favorite movie and why it is your favorite. Go!

[Let the partners attempt to share for 2 minutes.]

Discussion Question

• Partners who were sharing your favorite movie, how did it go? How did your partner treat you?

SAY: Please don't take what your partner did personally. I had instructed them to ignore you.

Discussion Questions

• How does it make you feel when you are trying to share something and the other person is not paying attention?

• Have you ever realized after a conversation (or during) that you were not being a good listener?

• How did that make you feel?

• What might poor listening communicate to the person sharing?

SAY: Now, I would like the students who were the "poor listeners" to go out of the room.

[Wait until all of the second group is out of hearing.]

SAY: When your partners return to the room, I will ask them to share an important moment from their past week. I want you to work really hard at being a good listener. Don't act forced or awkward in your listening but make appropriate eye contact and push aside distractions. You may ask follow-up questions to show interest, but don't make the time about you.

[Invite the other students back into the room.]

SAY: OK, the students who were just in the hallway will now be sharing. Share with your partner an important moment from your past week. Go!

[Allow the students to share for 2–3 minutes with their partners.]

Discussion Questions

• Group that was sharing, how did it go? How did your partner treat you?

• They were instructed to work at being good listeners. Did they do a good job?

• What did they do that displayed active listening?

• What could good listening communicate to the person sharing?

• What do you think good listening requires?

SAY: Listening is an essential skill in relationships. In a world of distractions, we must work hard to tune in to what others are saying and show others we care. Although we may not always think of prayer this way, listening is also a vital part of prayer. Let's explore this further.

- E X P L O R E -

Scripture on Elijah *10 minutes*

SAY: In a moment, we are going to read a section of Scripture. It is part of the story of the great prophet Elijah. Prophets were those chosen by God to deliver God's messages. Many times, prophets said things that were so challenging, their audience did not want to listen. We find Elijah hiding in a cave because he had challenged the prophets of Baal, a false God many worshipped, including the queen, Jezabel. He showed the prophets the power of God at Mt. Sinai while disproving Baal. Because of his boldness, his life was in danger. Elijah was frustrated because he felt that everyone had lost their way and they no longer followed God, and he was scared because he thought that he was alone.

Let's pick up the story now. Who'd be willing to read 1 Kings 19:3-13 aloud for us?

[Ask the volunteer to read the Scripture passage.]

Discussion Questions

• What did you notice about how God communicates at the end of this story?

SAY: The story says that God didn't come to Elijah in a booming voice or a great sign. God wasn't in the wind or the earthquake or the fire. God communicated through a "thin, quiet sound." Some translations say "a whisper" or a "still, small voice."

• Why, do you think, did God speak to Elijah in the quiet?

• What might this say about God?

[Allow the students to think about that for a moment.]

• Why, do you think, did Elijah hide his face in his coat when God did this?

SAY: We sometimes expect God to be revealed through miracles or great signs, but often God is found in the stillness. We may not hear an audible voice, but we can experience and sense God's presence in moments of quiet and reflection. But that is hard to do. Our lives are filled with noise and busyness. If we are honest, we are so used to the stimulus of our screens, it is hard for us to just breathe and listen for God.

Discussion Questions

• Where do you most often sense God?

• What helps you to get quiet and pray?

- R E F L E C T -

Meditating on God 10 minutes

SAY: Find a comfortable place in the room where you will be able to sit quietly to pray. It might be in a chair or on the floor. I will be giving some instructions throughout, so don't get so comfortable that you fall asleep.

[Allow the students time to get settled.]

SAY: Take a deep breath. Pay attention to your thoughts.

ASK: What is distracting you? What thoughts are filling your mind?

[Don't wait for answers.]

SAY: In the box provided in your Student Guide, write down everything that distracts you as you are attempting to focus.

[Allow 2 minutes for the students to journal.]

SAY: Now, quietly scribble over the distractions, covering them and allowing them to leave your mind.

SAY: As you keep your eyes closed, I will read the Lords Prayer and will pause after each verse. During these pauses, think about what that verse means to you and how you sense God in at that moment. Listen and be mindful.

[Read the Lord's Prayer aloud from Matthew 6:9-13 (following), pausing after each verse.]

⁹ Pray like this:
  Our Father who is in heaven,
      uphold the holiness of your name.
  ¹⁰ Bring in your kingdom
      so that your will is done on earth
      as it's done in heaven.
  ¹¹ Give us the bread we need for today.
  ¹² Forgive us for the ways we have wronged you,
      just as we also forgive those who have wronged us.
  ¹³ And don't lead us into temptation,
      but rescue us from the evil one.

SAY: Now turn to your Student Guide and journal a response to the questions in the Reflect section.

[Allow the students time to get settled.]

- CREATE -

The Sound of Silence 15 minutes

SAY: Who'd be willing to read aloud the instructions for the Create activity in your Student Guide?

[Ask the volunteer to read the instructions.]

SAY: Take about 10 minutes to complete this activity. Go!

[Allow about 10 minutes for the students to work on their own.]

SAY: Let's come back together and share our creations.

Discussion Questions

As Time Allows

• Who'd be willing to share your drawing?

• What did you like about this activity? What was challenging?

• How did this lesson help you think about God and prayer in a new way?

- N E X T -

Ideas to Try This Week

[Point out the ideas to try during the week.]

At home: Each day this week, take a moment to pray before you fall asleep and right after you wake up. Don't focus on saying anything to God. Use this space to simply be still and listen to what God is saying to you.

At school: Be extra observant this week at school. What do you notice happening around you? How can you pray for your friends, your classmates, and your teachers? Write down the names of the people you are praying for this week.

In your community: Walk to a park and sit under a tree. Psalm 46:10 says, "Be still, and know that I am God" (NIV). Use this Scripture as an elimination prayer, removing the final word or phrase each time you pray:

Be still, and know that I am God.
Be still, and know that I am.
Be still, and know.
Be still.
Be.

Unit 5: Our Theology

The things we believe as Christians, or our theology, are the foundational truths that empower us to understand the Christian faith with both our hearts and minds. This holistic understanding of our theology empowers us to share the principles of our faith in meaningful, purposeful ways. Over the next seven lessons, you will confirm what you may already know about Jesus, the Holy Spirit, and salvation, uncover new ways of understanding Christian thoughts around sin and grace, and enjoy the rich legacy that a life with Christ leaves for others to follow into eternity.

- C O N T E N T S -

Lesson 26

Looking Like God: The Imago Dei

LESSON DESCRIPTION: When discussing what it means to be "in the image of God," it is important to consider the varying expressions of what that looks like; cultur, gender, ethnicity, and social location all nuance what it means to be made in God's image. In this lesson, students will explore not only scriptural expressions of what it means to be made in God's image morally and spiritually, but also how the image of God (how we imagine God to look, how we imagine God to act, what God is concerned about, and so forth) shifts depending on a person's cultural and social experiences.

Lesson Outline

SECTION	TOPIC	DURATION
Connect	Unit 5 video: "Our Theology"	5 minutes
	Looking Like God	10 minutes
Explore	Where Is the Imago Dei?	15 minutes
Reflect	Your Name Here	15 minutes
Create	A God Portrait	15 minutes
Next	At home, at school, and in your community	Ideas to try this week

Supply List

Connect: Looking Like God
❏ Unit 5 video: "Our Theology"
❏ Paper (8.5 by 11)
❏ Writing utensils
❏ Colored pencils or markers
❏ Clear tape that is suitable for walls

Explore: Where Is the Imago Dei?
❏ Bibles (print or digital)
❏ Flip chart paper
❏ Marker

Reflect: Your Name Here
❏ Student Guides
❏ Writing utensils

Create: A God Portrait
❏ Student Guides
❏ Old magazines
❏ Scissors
❏ Glue

Next
❏ Student Guides

Confirm Teaching Plans

- C O N N E C T -

Video Time 5 minutes

SAY: We're going to begin this unit with a short video about our theology. Theology is our ongoing effort to reflect on who God is, what God does, and God's vision for humankind and all of creation.

[Show the Unit 5 introductory video: "Our Theology."]

Looking Like God 10 minutes

[Hand out paper and colored pencils or markers.]

SAY: We've heard that we are all made in God's image, but what does that really look like?

[Allow time for brief responses, if any.]

SAY: On the left side of the paper, write down ways that you think you are like God. Maybe you like to create things, just like God does. Or maybe you like to take care of people, like God does. Think of anything you can where you think you and God share a similar trait or interest.

[Allow a minute for students to list descriptions of themselves.]

SAY: On the right side, write down words that describe you physically. This can include your race, gender, hair and eye color, even your nationality.

[Allow a minute for students to list descriptions of themselves.]

SAY: Now, on the back of the paper, draw a picture of yourself using the physical traits you listed that also includes one of the traits that you and God share. Be creative.

[Allow a few minutes for students to draw their pictures.]

SAY: A lot of times when we think about God, we think of a big floating being in the clouds, or maybe just a booming voice and a bright light. In the book of Genesis, it says that God created humanity in God's own image. We bear the image of God even if we look different or come from different backgrounds. In some mystical and profound way, God looks like all of us. All of us are made in the image

Lesson 26

177

of God and certainly reflect attributes of God's character. Who wants to share your picture of what the image of God looks like in you?

[Give the students an opportunity to share their pictures. This is a great opportunity for both students and facilitator to learn about the backgrounds of the students. When complete, invite students to hang their pictures on a nearby wall with tape.]

- E X P L O R E -

Where Is the Imago Dei? 15 minutes

[**LEADER PREP:** Write on a flip chart the following Scripture references: Genesis 1:26-28; Genesis 2:7; Psalm 8:4-5; Romans 8:28-30.]

SAY: *Imago Dei.* Have any of you ever heard this phrase before? *Imago Dei* is a Latin phrase that means "image of God." This phrase comes from Genesis 1:27, which says, "God created humanity in God's own image, in the divine image God created them, male and female God created them." By definition, *Imago Dei* refers to how humans encompass the moral, spiritual, and intellectual elements of God. This means as humans, we have the ability to live out these characteristics of God. Whenever we read about a characteristic of God, we can rest assured that we embody those same characteristics.

There are a lot of texts that talk about the *Imago Dei.* We'll be focusing on four of them today. Before we dig into them more, we're going to read them aloud together. Who would like to read?

[Invite four students to read the focus texts aloud to the rest of the group: Genesis 1:26-28; Genesis 2:7; Psalm 8:4-5; and Romans 8:28-30.]

SAY: Thank you. Now we're going to dig into these texts and get a little more personal. We're going to gather in groups of four, and each person in the group will be assigned one of the four texts. First, each of you is going to read the text assigned to you aloud to your group; but when you come to a word like "man" or "him" or "humanity," you're going to insert your name. Once everyone in the group has done this, you're going to read your text aloud again, but this time you're going to insert the name of the person to your left for all of those words.

For example, when you read Genesis 2:7 aloud, it could say: "The LORD God formed Joshua from the topsoil of the fertile land and blew life's breath into Joshua's nostrils. Joshua came to life."

This will help us better understand how we are made in the image of God.

[Divide the students into groups. Make sure they know which verse they've been assigned. Allow 10 minutes to read through the Scriptures as a group. If they finish early, ask the students to read around the circle again, inserting a different name into the Scripture.]

- R E F L E C T -

Your Name Here *15 minutes*

SAY: Now turn to your Student Guide and journal your responses to the questions in the Reflect section of Lesson 26.

[Give the students time to respond to the Scripture reading by answering questions in their Student Guides. The text in the Student Guide says that they are to insert their name in the blanks of the Scripture passage.]

Discussion Questions

• How did it feel to hear your name in the text?

• What does this tell you about God?

• How did it feel to read the text with your friend's name in the text?

• What difference does it make when we use our names in the text? What does this tell you about the image of God?

- C R E A T E -

A God Portrait 15 minutes

SAY: Who'd be willing to read aloud the instructions for the Create activity in your Student Guide?

[Ask the volunteer to read the instructions.]

SAY: Take about 10 minutes to complete this activity. Go!

[Allow the students time to work on their own.]

SAY: Let's come back together and share our creations.

Discussion Questions As Time Allows

• Who'd like to share what you have created?

• What did you like about this activity? What was challenging?

• How did our lesson today inspire you to think or live differently?

- N E X T -

Ideas to Try This Week

[Point out the ideas to try during the week.]

At home: You are a reflection of the image of God to the world around you. Use a dry-erase marker and find a mirror you use at home. Write the words "Imago Dei: I am made in the image of God" as a reminder to reflect God's image to the world around you every day.

At school: Find your school's old yearbooks. Look through one from each decade for as far back as you can find. How have the images of students at your school changed over the years? How have they remained the same? What do you notice about the image of God when you look at these photos?

In your community: Psalm 19 reminds us that the heavens declare the glory of God. (You should probably look it up and read it for yourself.) Take a walk outside and look up. What parts of nature do you notice? What does this show you about the image of God?

Confirm Teaching Plans

Lesson 27
Hitting the Mark: Sin and Grace

LESSON DESCRIPTION: There are many definitions and understandings of sin. Some say that sin is breaking one of the Ten Commandments, while others say that sin is anything you do that is displeasing to God.

In this lesson, we will explore what it means to sin, its impact on self and others, and how love serves as the arrow to hit God's "target" of grace.

Lesson Outline

SECTION	TOPIC	DURATION
Connect	Lesson 27 video: "Hitting the Mark: Sin and Grace"	5 minutes
	What Is Sin?	15 minutes
Explore	The Wesleyan Quadrilateral	25 minutes
Reflect	Sin and Grace: Defined	5 minutes
Create	Grace Over Sin	15 minutes
Next	At home, at school, and in your community	Ideas to try this week

Supply List

Connect: What Is Sin?
❑ Lesson 27 video: "Hitting the Mark: Sin and Grace"
❑ Large sheets of paper or posterboard
❑ Marker

Explore: The Wesleyan Quadrilateral
❑ Copies of "The Wesleyan Quadrilateral" handout
❑ Writing utensils
❑ CEB Bibles
❑ Scenarios
❑ Projector (optional)
❑ Computer (optional)

Reflect: Sin and Grace: Defined
❑ Student Guides
❑ Writing utensils

Create: Grace Over Sin
❑ Student Guides
❑ Markers in dark and light colors

Next
❑ Student Guides

- C O N N E C T -

Video Time *5 minutes*

[**LEADER PREP:** Before beginning the lesson, make two signs: one that says "Believe" and the other "Don't Believe." Post the signs on opposite sides of the room. You will guide students through an activity where they identify with their beliefs about sin and grace.]

SAY: We use the word *sin* a lot in church, but often we don't do a very good job of explaining exactly what it is. Before we dig into the topic a little more, we're going to watch a short video that explores the question, "What is sin?"

[Show the video for Lesson 27.]

What Is Sin? *15 minutes*

SAY: We are going to try an activity about sin and grace. Please make a single-file line in the middle of the room.

[Wait for the students to line up.]

SAY: I have posted signs identifying one side of the room as "believe" and the other "don't believe." The middle of the room, where you are now, will be "not sure."

I am going to read several statements that we often hear about sin and grace. This is very important: These statements aren't right or wrong, but they do offer a variation of what many people in the Body of Christ believe. After you hear the statement, move to the side of the room that corresponds with what you believe about that statement.

Pay attention to a few things: (1) How long it takes you to decide where you may stand on a particular issue. (2) The ways in which people of the same faith can have varying opinions and interpretations of Scripture. Your decision to stand on one side of the room is not an indication of what you will always believe—just, based on your experiences and what you've learned, what you believe to be true today. Let's try a few practice statements.

[Use the practice statements below to get students accustomed to how the game works. Give enough time after reading each statement for students to move to a spot giving a clear response.

Confirm Teaching Plans

After each statement, suggest students pay attention to the range of responses. Most responses will have students sprinkled across the room. Other responses may have all students in one location.]

Practice Statements

1. Steph Curry is the best basketball player in the NBA.

2. Chocolate ice cream is the best flavor of ice cream.

SAY: Now for some statements about our lesson:

Statements

1. We are born into sin.

2. The Bible is irrefutable. It has no error in it.

3. Only when we break the Ten Commandments do we sin.

4. Sin affects only the person who committed the sin, not other people.

5. God always forgives us—no matter what.

6. We receive grace through Jesus Christ.

7. Our sins are forgiven as soon as we ask for forgiveness.

SAY: Isn't it amazing to see how we can all be a part of the same faith but have different understandings of sin and grace? There are many factors that determine how we view sin and grace—but more important, our experiences help us understand Jesus' relationship to us—and why his sacrifice on the Cross is so important.

- E X P L O R E -

The Wesleyan Quadrilateral
25 minutes

[**LEADER PREP:** Make a copy of the Quadrilateral handout for each student.]

[The students will use the Wesleyan Quadrilateral to consider ways sin and grace play a role in our lives as Christians. Use the formal explanation of the Wesleyan Quadrilateral below as a point of reference:

The Wesleyan Quadrilateral is made up of four "sides": (1) Scripture, (2) tradition, (3) reason, and (4) experience. For United Methodists, Scripture is considered the primary source and standard for Christian doctrine. Tradition is the time-honored witness of development and growth of the faith through the past centuries and in many nations and cultures. Experience is the individual's understanding and appropriating of the faith in the light of his or her own life. Through reason the individual Christian brings discerning and cogent thought to bear on the Christian faith. These four elements taken together bring the individual Christian to a mature and fulfilling understanding of the Christian faith and the required response of worship and service. (Source: *A Dictionary for United Methodists*, Alan K. Waltz, Copyright 1991 by Abingdon Press.)]

ASK: What do you remember about the Wesleyan Quadrilateral?

[Allow several students to respond.]

SAY: The Wesleyan Quadrilateral is made up of four different factors that we consider together in order to understand the Christian faith. John Wesley believed these four "sides" illuminated the core of Christian faith and helped us unpack the "whys" and "hows" of Christianity. What role do our experiences play in how we understand sin and grace? Does our intellect or educational experience have any impact on how we explore our faith? Wesley wanted us to consider these four things, Scripture, tradition, reason, and experience, in order to think through the ways in which we respond to Jesus and the world around us.

Sin and grace are often highly debated topics in the Christian faith, and learning how to not only understand sin and grace but also to navigate their affect on our lives and the lives of others.

[Give each student a copy of "The Wesleyan Quadrilateral" handout.]

SAY: For this next activity, I would like you to get into groups of two. We are going to think about how we would respond to some moral issues. First, I'd like to have three volunteers to read aloud the Scriptures about sin and grace listed on your handout.

[Ask the volunteers to read Genesis 2:15–3:13; Romans 3:23; and Romans 7:15-24.]

SAY: You have been given three scenarios on the worksheet.

[Read the scenarios.]

SAY: Now, work with your partner to write responses to the questions about each scenario.

What would you do in this situation?

Explain why you gave that answer using the Wesleyan Quadrilateral. Was it your understanding of Scripture that made you respond that way? Was it your life experiences or the tradition you're used to? Or was it an intellectual reason?

Work hard at giving thoughtful answers and provide explanations for your responses. In a few minutes, I will ask you to share your responses.

[Call on students to offer their responses. Repeat this until all scenarios are read or the allotted time is reached.]

- R E F L E C T -

Sin and Grace: Defined 5 minutes

SAY: Now turn to your Student Guide and journal in the Reflect section.

[Students will journal a one-sentence definition of the words *sin* and *grace* and answer the following questions: What is the relationship between sin and grace? When was a time that you experienced grace?]

- C R E A T E -

Grace Over Sin 15 minutes

SAY: Who'd be willing to read aloud the instructions for the Create activity in your Student Guide?

[Ask the volunteer to read the instructions.]

SAY: Take about 10 minutes to complete this activity. Go!

[Allow time for the students to work on their own.]

SAY: Let's come back together and share our creations.

Discussion Questions

As Time Allows

• Who'd like to share what you have created?

• What did you like about this activity? What was challenging?

• How did our lesson today inspire you to think or live differently?

- N E X T -

Ideas to Try This Week

[Point out the ideas to try during the week.]

At home: Each morning this week, read Romans 3:23-25 when you wake up. What does it feel like to be reminded of God's grace covering our sin every day?

At school: Who are the people who get on your nerves at school? Make it your goal to extend grace to them this week (and beyond!). What does extending grace to others teach you about the way God extends grace to you?

In your community: Look through your local newspaper. (In case you've never seen one, a newspaper is like an old-fashioned paper website.) Look for headlines and stories about hurt, pain, brokenness, and sin. Use a marker to write the word grace over each of theses stories. What would it look like for grace to cover sin in your community?

Confirm Teaching Plans

THE WESLEYAN QUADRILATERAL

SCRIPTURE	TRADITION
Scripture is considered the primary source and standard for Christian doctrine.	Tradition is the time-honored witness of development and growth of the faith through the past centuries and in many nations and cultures.
EXPERIENCE	**REASON**
Experience is the individual's understanding and appropriating of the faith in the light of his or her own life.	Through reason the individual Christian brings discerning and cogent thought to bear on the Christian faith.

SCRIPTURES FOR EXPLORATION
Genesis 2:15-3:13; Romans 3:23; Romans 7:15-24

	What would you do in this situation? Please explain.	What influenced your response: your understanding of Scripture, your life experiences, traditions, or intellectual reason? Please explain.
Scenario 1: A man's wife is sick and he cannot afford the medicine. Late one night, he breaks into a pharmacy and steals the medicine for her.		
Scenario 2: Your friend asks to copy your homework because he or she didn't do it the night before.		
Scenario 3: You come back from class and find that someone has broken into your locker and stolen your belongings.		

Lesson 28
Two Natures, One Man: Who Is Jesus?

LESSON DESCRIPTION: Understanding the complete nature of Jesus as fully human and fully divine is difficult. It requires us to explore the nature of paradoxes and the way our own lives are full of a variety of different roles and traits. An even deeper look into Jesus' life and ministry helps us better understand the ways our experiences make way for others to see Jesus in new and refreshing ways.

Lesson Outline		
SECTION	**TOPIC**	**DURATION**
Connect	One Body, Two Natures	15 minutes
Explore	Jesus: Fully Human, Fully Divine	20 minutes
Reflect	Jesus in Context	10 minutes
Create	An Illustrated Paradox	15 minutes
Next	At home, at school, and in your community	Ideas to try this week

Supply List

Connect: One Body, Two Natures
❑ Copies of the "One Body, Two Natures" handout
❑ Writing utensils
❑ Scissors

Explore: Jesus: Fully Human, Fully Divine
❑ Butcher paper
❑ Permanent markers
❑ CEB Bibles
❑ Journals or notebook paper
❑ Writing utensils
❑ Tape
❑ Dry-rease board or flip chart paper (optional)

Reflect: Jesus in Context
❑ Student Guides
❑ Writing utensils

Create: An Illustrated Paradox
❑ Student Guides
❑ Writing utensils

Next
❑ Student Guides

Confirm Teaching Plans

- C O N N E C T -

One Body, Two Natures *15 minutes*

[**LEADER PREP:** Make a copy of the "One Body, Two Natures" handout for each student. Also provide each student with pens and/or markers and scissors.]

SAY: When we think about who Jesus is, we can probably name a number of things: savior, teacher, Messiah, healer, etc. But to really dig into it, we must understand how Jesus was able to be both fully human and fully divine. It can be hard for some people to reconcile this idea that Jesus was God in the flesh; considering the ways we can have different aspects to our nature can help us understand how Jesus did as well.

[Hand out copies of the "One Body, Two Natures" handout.]

SAY: Notice that there is a line down the middle of the body outline on your handout. On both sides of the line write words that describe aspects of your nature that cannot be changed. For example, on one side you might write "brother" or "sister" or something related to your ethnicity, gender, or heritage. You might also include various character traits that are an important part of your nature, such as being humble or honest.

[Allow a few minutes for the students to fill both sides of the body outline with traits.]

SAY: Now cut the body in half on the dashed line. This should give you two halves of the body.

[Give the students time to cut the body outline in half along the line.]

SAY: When you think about the traits you wrote on your body outline, did any of them change once you divided the body into two? Whether the two body pieces are apart or together, each part contributes to the wholeness of who you are. This is how we can think about Jesus and who he is; he was fully human—a man who lived, learned, and engaged in community just like everyone else. He was also fully divine—God made in flesh who had the ability to heal, deliver, and be the perfect sacrifice for our sins. These two parts of Jesus' nature are inseparable.

Lesson 28

[Spend about 5 minutes discussing with the students the following questions.]

Discussion Questions

• What does it mean when we say that Jesus is fully human? Why is that important?

• What does it mean when you think about Jesus being fully divine?

• How does it change the way we think about Jesus when we remind ourselves that he had a physical body just like ours and was still God?

- E X P L O R E -

Jesus: Fully Human, Fully Divine *20 minutes*

[**LEADER PREP:** Before class, make a life-size body silhouette drawn on large butcher paper. Ask someone to lie down on the butcher paper and trace the person's body on the paper. Cut the life-size body silhouette into three sections. You may find it easier to make the silhouette from three sheets of butcher paper laid horizontally rather than vertically, drawing the head and shoulders on the top sheet, the torso and arms on the middle sheet (you might choose to make this sheet longer than the others so that the person can spread out his or her arms), and the legs and feet on the bottom sheet. On each respective part, write the Scriptures given in parentheses: Head and Shoulders (Mark 5:1-17; Mark 8:23-24); Torso and Arms (Luke 2:41-52; Luke 5:27-32); and Legs and Feet (John 1:1-18; John 14:8-11). Write these verses in small print, making sure to leave enough room for students to write responses around them. Give each group a section of the body; they will fill in what they learn about Jesus in their respective sections to reassemble the body at the end of the activity.]

SAY: Now let's divide into three groups.

[Give the students time to divide into three equal groups.]

SAY: To better understand how Jesus was fully human and fully divine, we turn to Scriptures that explore Jesus' life within these two

Confirm Teaching Plans

dimensions. Each group should have a section of the body with two Scripture references written on it.

Each group will read the biblical texts, and on your section of the body silhouette, write what you learned about Jesus. Here are some things I want you to think about as you read your Scriptures and fill in your portion of the body.

• What is happening in this Scripture that reveals parts of Jesus' nature?

• What does this Scripture tell us about Jesus as fully human and/or fully divine?

[You may choose to write these questions on a dry-erase board or flip chart so that students can refer to them during their Scripture exploration.]

SAY: When you've finished writing what you learned about Jesus, be prepared to give a brief summary of the texts you read and what you wrote on your section of the body.

[Give the students 5 minutes to write out what they've learned on their section of the body.]

SAY: Who wants to share what they learned first? When it's your turn to share, come up and tape your piece of the body on the wall. Remember, the whole purpose of the body is to work together.

[Let each group come up and present their brief summaries. When all groups are done, the entire body should be put back in the right order with all the pieces of Jesus clearly marked.]

SAY: How do we better understand who Jesus is now that we've been able to read about his life and literally piece it together? How is it that Jesus can be both fully human and fully divine?

[Allow time for answers.]

- R E F L E C T -

Jesus in Context *10 minutes*

SAY: Now turn to your Student Guide and journal a response to the questions provided.

The following is from the Student Guide:

Answer the following questions in your own words:

What does it mean to be fully human?

What does it mean to be fully divine?

What does it mean to be fully human and fully divine?

- C R E A T E -

An Illustrated Paradox 15 minutes

SAY: Who'd be willing to read aloud the instructions for the Create activity in your Student Guide?

[Ask the volunteer to read the instructions to the class.]

SAY: Take about 10 minutes to complete this activity. Go!

[Allow the students time to work on their own.]

SAY: Let's come back together and share our creations.

Discussion Questions
As Time Allows

• Who would like to begin and share what you created?

• What did you like about this activity? What was challenging?

• How did our lesson today inspire you to think or live differently?

- N E X T -

Ideas to Try This Week

[Point out the ideas to try during the week.]

At home: Share a summary of what you learned about Jesus being fully human and fully divine with your family. Ask them why they think this is important. For an extra challenge, invite them to draw their own illustrated paradoxes.

Confirm Teaching Plans

At school: The poet Walt Whitman once wrote, "I contain multitudes." What are the "multitudes" that you contain at school? How many different roles do you play in a given day? Pay attention to each one, inviting yourself to be fully you every time.

In your community: Take a walk at sunset. Pay attention to the world around you to notice moments that are fully human (garbage on the side of the street, traffic and noise) and fully divine (the wind blowing through the leaves, the sunset on the horizon). What does it mean to you to live in a world where you can experience both the human and the divine?

Lesson 28

ONE BODY, TWO NATURES

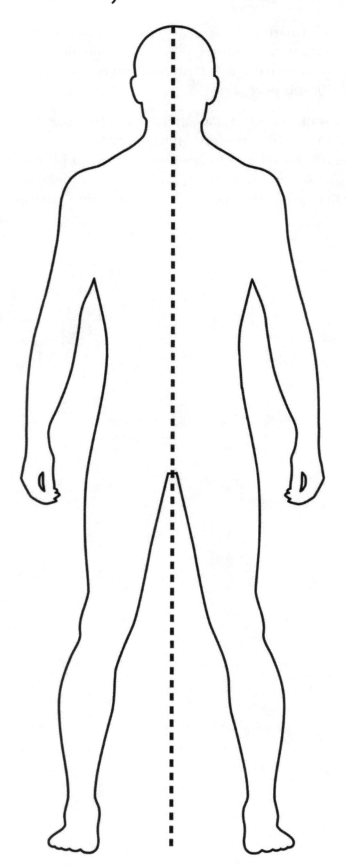

Lesson

29 What Is Salvation?

LESSON DESCRIPTION: Salvation is the gift we receive through Jesus Christ, but what is it and what purpose does it serve exactly? This lesson aims to define *salvation* and point us toward how it gives us access to God, how we can lean into the beauty of grace, and ways we can share the message of salvation and grace with others.

Lesson Outline		
SECTION	**TOPIC**	**DURATION**
Connect	The Five W's of Salvation	15 minutes
Explore	Scriptural Lifesavers	25 minutes
Reflect	Grace, Grace, Grace	5 minutes
Create	Was, Is, and Will Be	15 minutes
Next	At home, at school, and in your community	Ideas to try this week

Supply List

Connect: The Five W's of Salvation
❑ Copies of "The Five W's of Salvation" worksheet
❑ Writing utensils

Explore: Scriptural Lifesavers
❑ Copies of the "Scriptural Lifesavers" handout
❑ Writing utensils
❑ Bibles (digital or print)

Reflect: Grace, Grace, Grace
❑ Student Guides
❑ Writing utensils

Create: Was, Is, and Will Be
❑ Student Guides
❑ Writing utensils

Next
❑ Student Guides

- C O N N E C T -

The Five W's of Salvation 15 minutes

[**LEADER PREP:** Make copies of "The Five W's of Salvation" worksheet. You have been provided some lead-in questions for each "W" that can assist you in large-group discussion.]

SAY: *Salvation* — a word we have probably heard a million times; but what is it really? What does it mean to be "saved" and what purpose does it serve? We are going to work together to try and answer "The Five W's of Salvation" so we can get a better picture of what salvation is and how important it is to our lives.

[Give the students copies of "The Five W's of Salvation" worksheet and some writing utensils.]

SAY: We are going to work on this together because I think all of us have good answers to these questions. When we're done, we will have a big-picture idea of salvation that we can work from for the rest of our time together.

[Below are the leading questions for each *W*. Please feel free to expound on these questions to assist students in going the right direction.]

• Who offered us salvation?

• What is salvation? When thinking about our spirit, what does it mean to be "saved"?

• When did the act of salvation begin?

• Where did the act of salvation happen?

• Why did salvation happen?

Some suggested answers for each may be:

• Jesus Christ, God, God's plan, divine will

• It is the act of being saved from your sins; to be accepted by God

• On Calvary, at the Cross, when Jesus died, when Jesus was resurrected

• On Calvary, at the Cross, when Jesus died, when Jesus was resurrected

• Because God needed a plan to save us from our sin; because we were separated from God because of sin

- E X P L O R E -

Scriptural Lifesavers *25 minutes*

[**LEADER PREP:** Make copies of the "Scriptural Lifesavers" sheet. The number of copies is determined by whether you opt to give each group an entire sheet and assign each group one of the boxes (you'll make 6 copies) or you opt to cut the boxes out and give one to each group (you'll make 1 copy). The students will break into 6 groups, and you'll assign a box from the sheet to each group. The students will read the text(s) and answer the questions.]

SAY: We've spent a lot of time exploring what salvation is, who offered us salvation, when it happened, and why we need it. What we will find, however, is that salvation is experienced in different ways—this is why our salvation stories are often so unique! Because life leads us in many different ways, the ways we come to salvation and believing in Jesus are different.

Let's get into six groups. Try mixing up your groups with people you don't know or haven't had an opportunity to work with much.

[Give the groups the "Scriptural Lifesavers" sheet or cut-out boxes. If you have chosen to give each group the entire sheet, assign a number to each group.]

SAY: Every group should know which Scriptural Lifesaver is assigned to them. Now choose someone in your group to be your "researcher." This person will look up the Scriptures listed and read them aloud. Assign a "writer." This person will take notes on what you hear and answer the questions on your designated number. And pick someone to be your "reporter." This person will report your findings to the larger group. Make your choices now.

[Allow 1 minute for students to choose their roles.]

SAY: Take ten minutes to answer the questions on your sheet. Then we will reconvene and discuss.

[You may choose to collect answers on a flip chart paper or a dry-erase board, or explore responses in discussion form.]

Lesson 29

- R E F L E C T -

Grace, Grace, Grace 5 minutes

SAY: Now turn to your Student Guide and journal a response to the questions there.

The following is from the Student Guide:

Answer the following questions about grace:

• How would you explain grace to someone who had never heard of it before?

• What does it mean to you that God has been gracious toward you?

- C R E A T E -

Was, Is, and Will Be 15 minutes

SAY: Who'd be willing to read aloud the instructions aloud for the Create activity in your Student Guide?

[Ask the volunteer to read the instructions.]

SAY: Take about 10 minutes to complete this activity. Go!

[Allow about 10 minutes for the students to work on their own.]

SAY: Let's come back together and share our creations.

Discussion Questions As Time Allows

• Who would like to share what you created?

• What did you like about this activity? What was challenging?

• How did our lesson today inspire you to think or live differently?

- N E X T -

Ideas to Try This Week

[Point out the ideas to try during the week.]

At home: Go online and search for "salvation stories" or ask people to share their salvation stories on social media. How do these stories resonate with your own?

At school: Take a sticky note for each textbook you use at school and write, "Was saved, is saved, and will be saved" on each one. Place one of these sticky notes on the inside front cover of each book to remind you about God's salvation throughout the day.

In your community: We see God's salvation rooted in the Exodus narrative with God liberating God's people from oppression. When you look at your community and our world, where do you see oppression? Journal about what it would look like for God's salvation to offer liberation from this oppression. What can you do this week in your community to be a part of this liberation?

THE FIVE W'S
OF SALVATION

WHO offered salvation?	
WHAT is salvation? What does it mean to be "saved"?	
WHEN did the act of salvation begin?	
WHERE did the act of salvation happen?	
WHY did salvation happen?	

SCRIPTURAL LIFESAVERS

SCRIPTURAL LIFESAVER 1

A story of salvation

Luke 19:1-10

What does this passage say about salvation?

SCRIPTURAL LIFESAVER 2

A story of salvation

Luke 7:36-50

What does this passage say about salvation?

What does it add that was not said before?

SCRIPTURAL LIFESAVER 3

A story of salvation

John 3:16-21

What does this passage say about salvation?

What does it mean when it says "people loved darkness"?

What must people do for salvation?

SCRIPTURAL LIFESAVER 4

A story of salvation

John 4:7-30, 39-42

What does this passage say about salvation?

What made a difference in the belief of the people?

What does it add that was not said before?

SCRIPTURAL LIFESAVER 5

A story of salvation

John 10:7-10

What does this passage say about salvation?

What does it add that was not said before?

SCRIPTURAL LIFESAVER 6

A story of salvation

Ephesians 2:1, 4-10

What does this passage say about salvation?

What does it add that was not said before?

Lesson 30
Divine Helper: The Holy Spirit as Guide

LESSON DESCRIPTION: The Holy Spirit, one part of the triune nature of God, is a pivotal part of the Christian faith and understanding of Jesus' role in our lives. The Holy Spirit (or "Spirit of God," "Holy Ghost," or "Helper") has been a part of the Christian narrative since the beginning (Genesis 1). Understanding the Holy Spirit's place in our lives and how the Spirit's presence serves as a practical helper deepens our relationship with Christ and serves as an important reminder that God is always with us.

Lesson Outline

SECTION	TOPIC	DURATION
Connect	Hear My Voice	10 minutes
Explore	What Kind of Helper Is the Holy Spirit?	20 minutes
Reflect	I Ain't Afraid of No Ghost!	5 minutes
Create	Who You Gonna Call?	15 minutes
Next	At home, at school, and in your community	Ideas to try this week

Supply List

Connect: Hear My Voice
- ❑ Blindfolds, bandannas, or opaque pieces of cloth

Explore: What Kind of Helper Is the Holy Spirit?
- ❑ Copy of the "Holy Spirit Scriptures" sheet cut apart
- ❑ Flip chart paper
- ❑ Markers

Reflect: I Ain't Afraid of No Ghost!
- ❑ Student Guides
- ❑ Writing utensils

Create: Who You Gonna Call?
- ❑ Student Guides
- ❑ Writing utensils

Next
- ❑ Student Guides

Confirm Teaching Plans

- C O N N E C T -

Hear My Voice 10 minutes

[**LEADER PREP:** Prior to this activity, the room should be arranged like an obstacle course. This may mean scattering chairs, tables, or desks around the room, running rope or string across the room, or putting items such as balls, trashcans, or other objects in the walkway. Get creative!

A variation of this exercise might be having one student blindfolded while a team of students uses their voices to guide him or her to the destination. Another variation might be a team of three where one student is giving "right" directions and the other is giving "wrong" directions. The "right" and "wrong" voice could be one male and one female for differentiation.]

SAY: The Holy Spirit acts as a guide whenever we are in need of direction. Without the Holy Spirit speaking to us, guiding our thoughts and actions, we run the risk of running into things that can harm us or slow down our progress. Everyone partner up with someone. Decide which one of you will be the "voice" and which one will "follow the voice."

[Put a blindfold on the person who will be following the voice, and turn him or her in a circle three times.]

SAY: Now, on my "go," direct your partner across the room (or around an object). Listen carefully! You will hear the voices of other people around you so be mindful to listen closely. Your partner may call your name, give you directions to step left, right, over, and so forth. The person who reaches the other end of the room first, wins. Go!

Discussion Questions

• How easy was it to listen to the voice of your friend for guidance?

• At what point did it become more difficult?

• Did you find yourself needing to concentrate harder to hear the voice of only your guide versus the guide of another person?

[Allow time for answers.]

- E X P L O R E -

What Kind of Helper Is the Holy Spirit?

20 minutes

[**LEADER PREP:** Make copies of the "Holy Spirit Scriptures" sheet and cut it apart into slips.]

SAY: As we explore Scripture, you will notice that the Holy Spirit not only takes on different forms (rushing wind, fire, and so forth) but also is revealed to people in different ways. Have you ever said to yourself, "I had a feeling that was going to happen" or "Something told me to help this person"? That feeling or knowing is often the Holy Spirit speaking to us, nudging us to do or act in a certain way. Can anyone share a story of when something like this happened to you? How did you respond? Did you obey the feeling or ignore it?

[Allow time for 1-2 responses from students.]

SAY: We're going to break up into six groups and I'll be giving each group a slip of paper with a Scripture on it.

[Give each group a sheet of flip chart paper, a marker, and a "Holy Spirit Scriptures" slip.]

SAY: Scripture is our best place to look for examples of how the Holy Spirit helps and guides us. Every group should have a piece of chart paper, a marker, and the Scripture assigned to them. Take 6 to 7 minutes to read your Scripture and write down what the Holy Spirit is able to do for and/or with someone in the text. You may want to assign someone to read the Scripture, another person to point out examples, and another person to write them down on the paper. Be prepared to share your answers.

[After about 7 minutes, call the students back together.]

SAY: Let's go through each Scripture and see what kind of helper the Holy Spirit is. I bet we will see that the Holy Spirit not only helps in different ways but also reveals itself to people differently.

[Allow 5–6 minutes for group responses.]

Confirm Teaching Plans

These are the Holy Spirit Scriptures and the main point of each:

John 14:15-17, 25-27	Jesus promises to send the Holy Spirit.
Acts 1:8; 2:1-4	The Holy Spirit gives Jesus' followers power to witness and to carry on his ministry through the church.
Acts 8:29-31	The Holy Spirit guides people.
Romans 8:26-27	The Holy Spirit helps us in our weakness.
1 Corinthians 2:12-13	The Holy Spirit teaches those who are open to God.
1 Corinthians 12:4-7	The Spirit gives varieties of gifts for the common good.

- R E F L E C T -

I Ain't Afraid of No Ghost! 5 minutes

SAY: Now turn to your Student Guide and journal a response to the question there.

[Allow about 3 minutes for the students to journal their responses.]

ASK: How have you experienced the Holy Spirit in your life?

[Ask the volunteers to read their responses.]

- C R E A T E -

Who You Gonna Call? 15 minutes

SAY: Who'd be willing to read aloud the instructions aloud for the Create activity in your Student Guide?

[Ask the volunteer to read the instructions.]

SAY: Take about 10 minutes to complete this activity. Go!

[Allow about 10 minutes for the students to work on their own.]

SAY: Let's come back together and share our creations.

Lesson 30

Discussion Questions *As Time Allows*

• Who would like to share what you created?

• What did you like about this activity? What was challenging?

• How did our lesson today inspire you to think or live differently?

- N E X T -

Ideas to Try This Week

[Point out the ideas to try during the week.]

At home: The Greek and Hebrew words for "Spirit" also mean "breath." Find a quiet space where you won't be disturbed. Set a timer for five minutes (or longer) and just breathe. Don't focus on your thoughts but just focus on each breath in and out. What does this experience show you about the Holy Spirit?

At school: The Holy Spirit is our comforter and encourager. Choose three people at school and do something intentional this week to help comfort and encourage them. How do you feel the Holy Spirit with you and within you in these moments?

In your community: The Greek and Hebrew words for "Spirit" also mean "wind." Take a walk outside and pay attention to the air against your skin. Is it soothing? Refreshing? How does this natural sensation connect you with the Holy Spirit? Each time you feel the breeze whisper a prayer of "Thank you."

Confirm Teaching Plans

HOLY SPIRIT SCRIPTURES

JOHN 14:15-17, 25-27: [15] "If you love me, you will keep my commandments. [16] I will ask the Father, and he will send another Companion, who will be with you forever. [17] This Companion is the Spirit of Truth, whom the world can't receive because it neither sees him nor recognizes him. You know him, because he lives with you and will be with you....

[25] "I have spoken these things to you while I am with you. [26] The Companion, the Holy Spirit, whom the Father will send in my name, will teach you everything and will remind you of everything I told you.

[27] "Peace I leave with you. My peace I give you. I give to you not as the world gives. Don't be troubled or afraid."

ACTS 1:8; 2:1-4: [8] "Rather, you will receive power when the Holy Spirit has come upon you, and you will be my witnesses in Jerusalem, in all Judea and Samaria, and to the end of the earth."

[1] When Pentecost Day arrived, they were all together in one place. [2] Suddenly a sound from heaven like the howling of a fierce wind filled the entire house where they were sitting. [3] They saw what seemed to be individual flames of fire alighting on each one of them. [4] They were all filled with the Holy Spirit and began to speak in other languages as the Spirit enabled them to speak.

ACTS 8:29-31: [29] The Spirit told Philip, "Approach this carriage and stay with it."

[30] Running up to the carriage, Philip heard the man reading the prophet Isaiah. He asked, "Do you really understand what you are reading?"

[31] The man replied, "Without someone to guide me, how could I?" Then he invited Philip to climb up and sit with him.

ROMANS 8:26-27: [26] In the same way, the Spirit comes to help our weakness. We don't know what we should pray, but the Spirit himself pleads our case with unexpressed groans. [27] The one who searches hearts knows how the Spirit thinks, because he pleads for the saints, consistent with God's will.

1 CORINTHIANS 2:12-13: [12] We haven't received the world's spirit but God's Spirit so that we can know the things given to us by God. [13] These are the things we are talking about—not with words taught by human wisdom but with words taught by the Spirit—we are interpreting spiritual things to spiritual people.

1 CORINTHIANS 12:4-7: [4] There are different spiritual gifts but the same Spirit; [5] and there are different ministries and the same Lord; [6] and there are different activities but the same God who produces all of them in everyone. [7] A demonstration of the Spirit is given to each person for the common good.

Lesson 31
What's Next: Life After Death

LESSON DESCRIPTION: The hope of a life with Jesus Christ after death is one of the beautiful promises that we have as Christians. There are many depictions and explanations of what life will be like after we die—many of these depictions are seen in the media, literature, and other art forms. While we cannot know in advance of Jesus' return or how the world will end, we can be sure that loving God and right actions on earth set us up to spend eternity with Jesus.

Lesson Outline

SECTION	TOPIC	DURATION
Connect	What Does Heaven Look Like?	10 minutes
	Lesson 31 video: "What's Next: Life After Death"	5 minutes
Explore	The Good News	20 minutes
Reflect	The Next Place	15 minutes
Create	Heaven: Coming Soon to an Earth Near You!	15 minutes
Next	At home, at school, and in your community	Ideas to try this week

Supply List

Connect: What Does Heaven Look Like?
- ❑ Lesson 31 video: "What's Next: Life After Death"
- ❑ Flip chart paper
- ❑ Marker
- ❑ Tape

Explore: The Good News
- ❑ Flip chart paper
- ❑ Markers
- ❑ Sticky notes
- ❑ Bibles
- ❑ Writing utensils

Reflect: The Next Place
- ❑ Student Guides
- ❑ Writing utensils

Create: Heaven: Coming Soon to an Earth Near You!
- ❑ Student Guides
- ❑ Colored pencils

Next
- ❑ Student Guides

- C O N N E C T -

What Does Heaven Look Like? 10 minutes

[**LEADER PREP:** Place a sheet of flip chart paper on a wall or the board in front of the class. Draw a line down the center. Label the left side "Heaven" and the right side "The End of the World."

SAY: Today we're going to talk about two subjects that can be confusing, heaven and the end of the world. Before we get into what the Bible has to say about these subjects, let's spend a few minutes thinking about ways that our culture talks about these two ideas. First, when you think of heaven, what comes to mind? How is heaven depicted in movies, in music, or on TV shows that you watch?

[Give the students a chance to respond for 2 or 3 minutes.]

SAY: What about the end of the world? What immediately comes to mind when someone mentions that? How have you seen it depicted?

[Give the students another 2 or 3 minutes to respond.]

SAY: Thanks for all those answers! We're going to watch a short video now to explain a little more about what we'll be talking about today.

Video Time 5 minutes

[Show Lesson 31 video: "What's Next; Life After Death."]

- E X P L O R E -

The Good News 20 minutes

[**LEADER PREP:** Place two pieces of chart paper on the front wall. Divide each paper in half and label the four columns with the following verses: Matthew 25:31-46; Romans 8:35–9:1; 2 Peter 3:8-14; and Revelation 21:1-8.]

SAY: We're going to take a look now at what the Bible says about two related, but distinct topics: life after death and the end times. While the topics are very different, they share one common question that we all wonder about: What happens next? To explore this, we're going to break into four groups. Each group is going to be assigned one of the passages listed at the front of the room.

When we talk about the end times, what we're really talking about is the Second Coming of Jesus. In the Gospels we're told that the coming of Jesus is good news for the world. For our discussion today we aren't going to focus on the why or the how of the Second Coming, instead we're going to focus on where we find the good news in these verses.

You'll have one member of your group read the verses aloud and then, as a group, you'll brainstorm answers to the question, "What is the good news here?" Write your answers down on sticky notes and then come and place them on the chart paper under your Scripture reference. Do you have any questions?

[Assign each group a passage. Give the students seven or eight minutes to read the passage and brainstorm answers to the assigned question. When it's almost time to reconvene, remind them to place their sticky notes on the chart paper.]

SAY: Let's talk about the good news we found in these verses.

[Read off some of the answers from the Matthew group, then the Romans group, and so forth.]

SAY: What are some of the common themes you hear after reading through the different groups' answers? What thread ties all these verses together?

[Give the students an opportunity to answer.]

SAY: It's important to talk about concepts like life after death or the end times because as we said earlier, these topics can be scary and anxiety inducing. What are some ways you think we can talk about death or heaven that would make our conversations more honest and less scary or frustrating?

[Give the students time to answer the question. If someone has an interesting insight, ask the rest of the class whether they agree or disagree or have something they'd like to add.]

- REFLECT -

The Next Place 15 minutes

SAY: Now turn to your Student Guide and journal your responses to the questions in the Reflect section of Lesson 31.

[Give the students time to respond to the questions in their Student Guides.]

Discussion Questions

• What, do you think, happens after we die?

• How would you describe the "new heaven" and "new earth"?

- C R E A T E -

Heaven: Coming Soon to an Earth Near You!

15 minutes

SAY: Who'd be willing to read aloud the instructions for the Create activity in your Student Guide?

[Ask the volunteer to read the instructions.]

SAY: Take about 10 minutes to complete this activity. Go!

[Allow the students time to work on their own.]

SAY: Let's come back together and share our creations.

Discussion Questions As Time Allows

• Who'd like to share what you have created?

• What did you like about this activity? What was challenging?

• How did our lesson today inspire you to think or live differently?

- N E X T -

Ideas to Try This Week

[Point out the ideas to try during the week.]

At home: Have a conversation with your family this week and ask them what they think happens when someone dies. Ask them what they think the "new heavens and the new earth" will be like and share with them some of the things you learned in your confirmation class.

At school: Write a letter to a friend at school, sharing with that person one thing you learned about heaven in your confirmation class. Ask your friend to share with you one thought or question he or she has about heaven or about life after death.

In your community: Rather than waiting around to go to heaven someday, we are invited to help bring heaven to earth each and every day. Talk to your pastor or other community leaders about ways that you can volunteer to help make the world around you a better place. Invite your family or your friends to spend a day volunteering together. What does this experience show you about the "new heavens and the new earth"?

Lesson 32

From Whence We Came: The Creeds

LESSON DESCRIPTION: In order to understand our walk as United Methodist Christians, we must delve into the historical development of our faith. This lesson will introduce students to the creeds of the Christian faith as directives that guide and shape the modern interpretations and expressions of our beliefs.

Lesson Outline

SECTION	TOPIC	DURATION
Connect	Relay Race	15 minutes
Explore	The Relay of Faith	20 minutes
Reflect	Documenting History	5 minutes
Create	Credo	15 minutes
Next	At home, at school, and in your community	Ideas to try this week

Supply List

Connect: Relay Race
- ❏ Balloons
- ❏ Large bucket
- ❏ Bibles

Explore: The Relay of Faith
- ❏ Copies of the "Creed Cards"
- ❏ Copies of the *United Methodist Hymnal*

Reflect: Documenting History
- ❏ Student Guides
- ❏ Writing utensils

Create: Credo
- ❏ Student Guides
- ❏ Writing utensils

Next
- ❏ Student Guides

- C O N N E C T -

Relay Race 15 minutes

[Place a bucket for the balloons on one side of the room so that students will have enough space to run to it.]

SAY: In many Olympic games, the passing of the baton is an important team exercise in not only trusting your teammates, but trusting that what they are passing on to you will help you reach the finish line.

[Assign students into two teams. You can divide the teams by having students count off 1, 2, 1, 2 until divided evenly. If the teams are not even, you can appoint a student to serve as the judge.]

SAY: In your teams, you will be responsible for helping your team fill this bucket with balloons. One of you will blow up the balloon (and yes, it has to be fully inflated, no cheating), the next student will tie the balloon, and the third student will run with the balloon between his or her knees to the bucket and place the balloon in the bucket with his or her hands. Choose who on your team will do each part— the rest of you can cheer your team on to victory! The first team to get all ten balloons in the bucket wins.

[Give each team 10 balloons. On your say, students will blow up, tie, and run the balloons to the bucket. Encourage the students to cheer their teammates on throughout the game.]

SAY: Wow! What an intense game! So let's talk about this.

Discussion Questions

• What would you say made the winning team successful?

• What difficulties do you think made winning hard? Did anyone or anything get in the way of your success?

• How important was it to have people around you cheering you on?

• How important is it for everyone to have the same goal and intentions when completing a task?

SAY: Let's read aloud together Hebrews 12:1-2, a text that shows us what it means to run a race together.

[Ask the entire class to read the text together.]

- E X P L O R E -

The Relay of Faith 20 minutes

[*LEADER PREP:* Make copies of the "Creed Cards" handout, which includes the Apostles' Creed and the Nicene Creed. You may choose to make copies of each creed card for students to keep in their purses or wallets for easy access after this lesson. You will also need access to *The United Methodist Hymnal*, specifically pages 880–889, which contain a number of other affirmations of faith for your class to discuss.]

SAY: Just like we have relay games that involve everyone's participation to meet our goal, we also have a relay of faith that is passed on from person to person until all are introduced to Jesus and the Christian faith. The creeds are a way that the church can pass along its "statement of faith" from generation to generation.

Earlier in this study, we explored what we believed – what it means to be saved, how grace plays a role in our Christian development. The creeds tell us the basics of what Christians have believed throughout the centuries. Having that connection to the past helps us better understand our present and future in Christ.

We have many different creeds, and each is unique. Often, creeds were written to deal with issues that were in dispute. You can sometimes tell why a creed was written by what is in it and by how much space it devotes to a particular topic. For example, the big issue in the Apostles' Creed is "Who is Jesus?" The paragraph on Jesus is bigger than the rest of the creed. Each creed emphasizes specific concepts.

In The United Methodist Church, we have use a variety of creeds that summarize our faith instead of just one. Let's look at a few of them.

[Divide the students into groups of 3 to 5 each. Make sure each group has a copy of the Apostles' Creed, the Nicene Creed, or one of the "Affirmations of Faith" found in *The United Methodist Hymnal*.]

SAY: With your group, read aloud the creed you've been assigned and answer the following questions:

- What is the creed trying to emphasize? Does it repeat itself on particular topics?

- What about the creed you read did you find confusing or unexpected? Why?

- Did the creed cause you to think about any ideas you hadn't considered before?

   [Give the students 7 or 8 minutes to read through the assigned creeds and answer these questions, then gather the students back into the larger group.]

ASK: What did you find most interesting about your conversations? What about the creeds surprised you?

- R E F L E C T -

Documenting History *5 minutes*

SAY: Now turn to your Student Guide and journal a response to the questions there.

   [Allow the students 2 to 3 minutes to answer the questions in their Student Guides.]

Discussion Questions

- How does learning about the history of a movement teach you about where it is going?

- What words or phrases from the creeds do you connect with most? Why?

Confirm Teaching Plans

- CREATE -

Credo *15 minutes*

SAY: Who'd be willing to read aloud the instructions aloud for the Create activity in your Student Guide?

[Ask the volunteer to read the instructions.]

SAY: Take about 10 minutes to complete this activity. Go!

[Allow about 10 minutes for the students to work on their own.]

SAY: Let's come back together and share our creations.

Discussion Questions
As Time Allows

• Who'd like to share what you created?

• What did you like about this activity? What was challenging?

• How did our lesson today inspire you to think or live differently?

- NEXT -

Ideas to Try This Week

[Point out the ideas to try during the week.]

At home: Go online and post one of your credo statements on social media. Invite your friends online to do the same!

At school: Visit your school library and ask where you can learn more about the history of your school. What does learning about where your school has been teach you about where your school is today and where it is going in the future?

In your community: Who has lived in your neighborhood the longest? Visit them and ask how they have seen the neighborhood grow and evolve over time. What has remained the same? What has been lost along the way? And what new things do they notice emerging?

CREED CARDS

THE APOSTLES' CREED

I believe in God, the Father almighty,
    creator of heaven and earth.

I believe in Jesus Christ, God's only Son, our Lord,
    who was conceived by the Holy Spirit,
    born of the Virgin Mary,
    suffered under Pontius Pilate,
    was crucified, died, and was buried;
    he descended to the dead.
    On the third day he rose again;
    he ascended into heaven,
    he is seated at the right hand of the Father,
    and he will come to judge the living and the
        dead.

I believe in the Holy Spirit,
    the holy catholic* Church,
    the communion of saints,
    the forgiveness of sins,
    the resurrection of the body,
    and the life everlasting. Amen.

universal

THE NICENE CREED

We believe in one God,
    the Father, the Almighty,
    maker of heaven and earth,
    of all that is, seen and unseen.

We believe in one Lord, Jesus Christ,
    the only Son of God,
    eternally begotten of the Father,
    God from God, Light from Light,
    true God from true God,
    begotten, not made,
    of one Being with the Father;
    through him all things were made.
For us and for our salvation
    he came down from heaven,
    was incarnate of the Holy Spirit and the
      Virgin Mary
    and became truly human.
    For our sake he was crucified under
      Pontius Pilate;
    he suffered death and was buried.*
    On the third day he rose again
    in accordance with the Scriptures;
    he ascended into heaven
    and is seated at the right hand of the Father.
    He will come again in glory
    to judge the living and the dead,
    and his kingdom will have no end.

We believe in the Holy Spirit, the Lord, the
      giver of life,
    who proceeds from the Father and the Son,
    who with the Father and the Son
      is worshiped and glorified,
    who has spoken through the prophets.
    We believe in one holy catholic** and
      apostolic church.
    We acknowledge one baptism
      for the forgiveness of sins.
    We look for the resurrection of the dead,
      and the life of the world to come. Amen.

*Traditional use of this creed includes these words: "He descended into hell."
**universal*

Unit 6: Our Faith and Calling

Our faith and the living out of our faith are intricately linked. James 2:17 says, "In the same way, faith is dead when it doesn't result in faithful activity." Living out our faith clarifies our calling and strengthens our relationship with God. As our relationship with God grows, and we better understand our calling, our faith becomes even deeper. We cannot fully understand either faith or calling without the other. This unit will challenge teens to put together all they have been learning over the past sessions and articulate what they believe in their own words. They will be pushed to take seriously their faith and discipleship through realistic examination of the United Methodist baptismal vows and the living out of those vows within the life of their congregation. Ultimately, each teen will have to decide for himself or herself if being confirmed in The United Methodist Church is a calling he or she is willing and able to accept.

- CONTENTS -

Lesson

33 A Faith to Decide

LESSON DESCRIPTION: Making decisions is a part of everyday life. Some decisions we make without much thought such as oatmeal or cereal for breakfast. Others may require more thought and intentionality, such as how to respond to an antagonistic coworker. Rarely do our everyday decisions hold life-changing consequences in the balance. The decision to follow Christ is both a major life-changing decision and an everyday decision. Our initial "I will follow" response to Christ becomes the foundation upon which all other decisions are built. That first "yes" is the driving force behind who we will be and how we will interact with the world. This lesson is intended to help teens consider what following Christ looks like for them in both life-changing and day-to-day ways. Teens will explore the decision-making process of several of Jesus' disciples and the implications those decisions had for their lives. They will also review their emotions from the beginning of the *Confirm* journey and compare them to the emotions they are currently experiencing. Ideally this refection will provide perspective as they approach making a decision about confirmation.

Lesson Outline

SECTION	TOPIC	DURATION
Connect	Would You Rather?	10 minutes
	Unit 6 video: "Our Faith and Calling"	5 minutes
Explore	Which Way Did He Go?	20 minutes
Reflect	Documenting Emotions	5 minutes
Create	Dear Disciple	15 minutes
Next	At home, at school, and in your community	Ideas to try this week

Supply List

Connect: Would You Rather?
❏ Unit 6 video: "Our Faith and Calling"

Explore: Which Way Did He Go?
❏ Copies of the "Which Way Did He Go?" handout
❏ Writing utensils

Reflect: Documenting Emotions
❏ Student Guides
❏ Writing utensils

Create: Dear Disciple
❏ Student Guides
❏ Writing utensils

Next
❏ Student Guides

- C O N N E C T -

Would You Rather? *10 minutes*

[You will be reading a list of eight options for your teens to choose between. With each option, the teens will need to take a step either forward or backward. For choices 5–8, please ask the teens to close their eyes so that they cannot see how others in the group answer the questions. This is for conversation's sake. The options will not be overly invasive or sensitive so as to make teens feel uncomfortable. You may need to remind the teens to take normal-size steps when selecting an option.]

SAY: Please stand side by side in a single-file line in the middle of the room. For each question, there will be an Option A and an Option B. If you would rather choose Option A, take one step forward. If you would rather choose Option B, take one step backward. After each choice, you will move from where you were after the previous statement.

[Read the following statements out loud, pausing until all of the students have moved a step forward or backward.]

So, with your eyes open: Would you rather…

1. (A) Bananas and peanut butter *OR* (B) Celery and peanut butter?

2. (A) Be tiny as a stamp *OR* (B) Big as a skyscraper?

3. (A) Big group of people *OR* (B) By yourself?

4. (A) Sit on the bench *OR* (B) Sit in the stands?

Now, with your eyes closed: Would you rather…

5. (A) Super smart *OR* (B) Super rich?

6. (A) First pew *OR* (B) Last pew?

7. (A) Hungry *OR* (B) Thirsty?

8. (A) Total darkness *OR* (B) Blinding light?

SAY: OK, you may open your eyes and sit down right where you are.

Discussion Questions

• Do you think that you responded to the questions in a different way with your eyes closed than you did when they were open?

• Did being able to see how others were answering affect your decision-making? How so?

• When making decisions in real life, how much, do you think, do the opinions of others influence you?

Video Time *5 minutes*

SAY: For the next several lessons, we are going to be focusing on decisions and decision-making. We have a short video that's going to give us a little insight into what kind of decisions I'm talking about.

[Show the Unit 6 introductory video: "Our Faith and Calling."]

SAY: Your decision to be confirmed or follow Christ isn't simply about behaving a certain way, knowing the right things, or meeting a certain set of expectations. As we walk though these last stages of confirmation, we hope you will come to understand better that deciding to follow Christ is a journey of experiencing God's grace, hope, and love in unimaginable ways. And we hope that you will decide to follow Christ and become an agent of God's grace, hope, and love in unimaginable ways.

Our first step on this part of the journey is to look at the lives of three different disciples and their decisions to follow Jesus. Hopefully, this will help you to have a better understanding of the variety of decisions people are confronted with when choosing to follow Jesus.

- EXPLORE -

Which Way Did He Go? *20 minutes*

[*LEADER PREP:* Make copies of the "Which Way Did He Go?" handout. IMPORTANT: If you have a group of 15 or fewer, divide the students into three groups that are about the same size. For larger groups, divide the students into 6 or 9 groups, assigning each group one of the disciples (Peter, Thomas, or John).]

SAY: We are going to divide into three* (or six or nine) groups. Group 1 is assigned Peter, Group 2 Thomas, and Group 3 John. The passages for your disciple are listed on this handout.

[Distribute the "Which Way Did He Go?" handouts. Direct the student's attention to the questions as a resource for shaping their biography statements.]

SAY: These passages refer to incidents where each of these disciples had a decision to make. After reading all the passages about their decisions, brainstorm as a group how you would describe your disciple based on his decision-making.

Then together, answer the biography questions to make a profile of your disciple. You have about 10 minutes to complete this. Go!

[Allow the groups to take 10 minutes to work on their biographies.]

SAY: Now, let's go around the group and share our biographies.

[After teams have shared their bios, discuss comparisons between the disciples' decisions and the teens' decision to follow Jesus, using the questions below.]

Discussion Questions

• What can we learn from these three disciples about deciding to follow Jesus?

• In what ways was easier for the disciples to follow Jesus than it is for us?

• In what ways is it easier for us to follow Jesus that in was for the disciples?

SAY: There were multiple points in each of these disciples' lives when they had to make a decision to follow Jesus. Sometimes it seemed like it was easy for them to say "Yes, I will follow"—they just dropped everything and left. Other times, it was not so clear, because saying "yes" would put their very lives at stake. Each of these men must have experienced a variety of emotions as they said yes to being a disciple of Jesus Christ. We began our journey together taking considerable time to examine our feelings as we started this decision-making process. Now you are going to take a little bit of time to reevaluate what you are feeling now that we are approaching the end.

- R E F L E C T -

Documenting Emotions *5 minutes*

SAY: You are now going to have the opportunity to think more deeply about which of these disciples you connect with and how the choices he made can help as you make your own decisions.

To do that, I'm going to ask you to take a look back at the "sticky notes" you created during our very first session, Traveling Together (Unit 1, Lesson 1). This is at the very front of your Student Guide.

> [Give the students 30 seconds to a minute to look back at what they wrote in the Reflect section of Lesson 1.]

SAY: Now turn to today's lesson in your Student Guide, and journal a response to the questions there.

> [Give the students 2 minutes to answer the questions in the Student Guide. Then ask for a couple volunteers to share their responses to the following questions from the Student Guide.]

Discussion Questions

• How are you feeling about ending confirmation?

• Which of the three disciples (Peter, Thomas, or John) do you connect with most? Why?

- C R E A T E -

Dear Disciple *15 minutes*

SAY: Who'd be willing to read aloud the instructions aloud for the Create activity in your Student Guide?

> [Ask the volunteer to read the instructions.]

SAY: Take about 10 minutes to complete this activity. Go!

> [Allow the students time to work on their own.]

SAY: Let's come back together and share our creations.

Discussion Questions *As Time Allows*

• Who'd like to share what you have created?

• What did you like about this activity? What was challenging?

• How did our lesson today inspire you to think or live differently?

- N E X T -

Ideas to Try This Week

[Point out the ideas to try during the week.]

At home: Invite your family to read James 2:14-18 together. Have each member of your family write down one way that you can make more faithful decisions in your life.

At school: Every day this week pray for someone you do not get along with very well at school. Don't pray for yourself, but be intentional about praying for that person. At the end of the week, reflect on how you feel toward him or her.

In your community: Who makes the decisions that impact your community? Go online and research your city officials and council people. Reach out to the ones who represent your neighborhood and ask them about the process they use to make big and small decisions.

WHICH WAY DID HE GO?

PETER: Matthew 4:18-19; 14:22-33; 16:13-20; 17:1-9; 19:23-29; 26:31-46, 69-75; John 21:15-19

THOMAS: Matthew 10:1-4; 19:23-29; John 11:4-16; 14:1-7; 20:24-28; Acts 1:12-14

JOHN: Matthew 4:21-22; 17:1-9; 19:23-29; 26:36-46; Mark 10:35-45; John 19:25-27;
   20:1-9; 21:1-8, 20-25

Biography Questions

1. How did his decisions shape the way he followed Jesus?

2. What was his relationship with Jesus like?

3. How did Jesus respond to his questions?

4. How did he respond to Jesus' questions?

5. What emotions do you think this disciple felt?

Lesson
34 A Faith to Confirm

LESSON DESCRIPTION: As the teens approach confirmation, this lesson will give them a time to explore the professions they will be asked to make and the ramifications of that profession of faith in their lives. With the help of John Wesley and Zacchaeus, the teens will see that there are a variety of ways proclaim Christ's Lordship and will be encouraged that God's grace covers us when we fall short on keeping our end of the promise to sin, its impact on self and others, and how love serves as the arrow to hit God's "target" of grace.

Lesson Outline		
SECTION	**TOPIC**	**DURATION**
Connect	Tweet Your Belief	15 minutes
	Lesson 34 video: "A Faith to Confirm"	5 minutes
Explore	Big Faith	20 minutes
Reflect	Saying 'I Do'	5 minutes
Create	What Was He Thinking?	15 minutes
Next	At home, at school, and in your community	Ideas to try this week

Supply List

Connect: Tweet Your Belief
❏ Half-sheets of paper
❏ Pre-written Scripture reference slips of paper (1 for each student)
❏ Pre-written tweet questions on posterboard
❏ Bibles
❏ Writing utensils
❏ Posterboard (1 per group)
❏ Markers
❏ Tape
❏ Lesson 34 video: "A Faith to Confirm"

Explore: Big Faith
❏ Copies of the "Big Faith" handout
❏ Student Guides
❏ Writing utensils

Reflect: Saying 'I Do'
❏ Student Guides
❏ Writing utensils

Create: What Was He Thinking?
❏ Student Guides
❏ Writing utensils

Next
❏ Student Guides

- C O N N E C T -

Tweet Your Belief 15 minutes

[**LEADER PREP:** Write the following Scripture references on slips of paper. Include the letter references A–E. Create as many slips of paper as there are teen participants. NOTE: If you do not have enough participants to create 5 groups of at least 2 teens, then use only the passages A–C, creating at least 3 groups of 2 teens. Also write on posterboard the 3 questions that follow. Make the poster visible only once you reach that portion of the activity.]

A. John 4:39-42   B. Romans 10:9-13

C. 1 John 4:7-16   D. 2 Corinthians 4:13-14

E. Philippians 3:7-14

1. What does the Scripture say about professing Jesus as Lord and Savior?

2. What impact does a person's profession of faith in Jesus have on others?

3. What difference does professing your faith in Jesus make in everyday life?

   [Mix up the slips of paper in a bowl and ask teens to draw out one slip for themselves.]

SAY: Please stand. Each of you has received a slip of paper with a Scripture reference on it. You have 30 seconds to find all the other people in the room with the same Scripture reference as you. Once your group has gathered together, find a place to sit together.

   [Allow enough time for the students to assemble into groups.]

SAY: Now, you have 10 minutes to read the passage and do two things. Listen carefully.

1. Write your passage on a poster. Include the letter a–E given on the slips. You may add some color to it, but don't spend too much time on this.

2. Then summarize your passage in a tweet (140 characters or less). Pick one of these questions to answer as the focus of your tweet. I have listed them here for you.

[Reveal the poster on which you have written the 3 questions. Read the questions aloud.]

SAY: Write your tweet on a piece of paper and be ready to share it with the group.

[Hang up the posters around the room so that they are clearly visible for all students. Allow the students time to write their tweets.]

SAY: Turn over your slip of paper and list the numbers 1–5 down the left side of the slip. Each of your posters is marked with a letter, A–E. As each group reads its tweet, write down the letter of the passage you think it is describing beside that number. At the end, we will see who got the most correct and is an excellent interpreter of tweets! Obviously, you will get your own group correct!

[After you have determined who had the most correct tweets, have one person from each group read his or her group's Scripture passage followed by the summary tweet. Ask another person from each group to write their tweet on the poster associated with their passage. Keep the posters up for the remainder of the lesson.]

Discussion Questions

• How can condensing as many as 10 verses of Scripture into 140 characters be helpful for professing your faith?

• Can you think of any problems that condensing 10 verses of Scripture into 140 characters might cause? If so, what or why is it a problem?

• Do you notice any consistent themes or similarities in these "tweets" about professing faith in Jesus? If so, what are they?

Video Time 5 minutes

SAY: Professing faith in Jesus as Lord and Savior is the foundation for a journey with God. However, making that profession and understanding what it is you are saying you believe can be confusing. We are going to watch a short video about the struggle of the founder of Methodism, John Wesley, to profess and believe that Jesus died for his sins, forgave him, loved him, and gave him eternal life.

[Show the Lesson 34 video: "A Faith to Confirm."]

- E X P L O R E -

Big Faith *20 minutes*

[*LEADER PREP:* Make copies of the "Big Faith" handout for every student.]

SAY: By finding assurance in God's love for him, Wesley gained the confidence to help others grow in their love of God by setting some guiding principles (later called rules) for them to follow. Wesley encouraged fellow believers to (1) do no harm, by avoiding evil, (2) do good, and (3) constantly connect with God. These general rules influence our current membership vows. At the beginning of our journey together, we briefly looked at the membership vows you will take at confirmation. We focused on the importance of the vow to support our church by our "prayers, presence, gifts, service, and witness."

We are now going to return to the first three of the membership vows that focus on your personal commitment to Jesus Christ. If you choose to be confirmed, then the pastor is going to ask you three very important questions. May I have three volunteers to will read these questions?

[Refer the volunteers and the rest of the class to the Reflect section of the Student Guide. Then have each volunteer read one of the membership vows.]

SAY: These three questions are basic guidelines to claiming that Jesus is your Lord and Savior. If you choose to answer "I do" to each of these questions, then you are choosing to accept responsibility for your own faith.

• By responding "I do" to the first vow, you are admitting that there are people, places, and activities that keep you from loving God and your neighbor and that cause you to sin. You are accepting responsibility to turn away from and not engage in those things anymore.

• By responding "I do" to the second vow, you are recognizing that God gives you a choice to be in a relationship with God and fellow believers. You are promising to willingly walk away from any person, place, thing, or system that separates you from God or does harm to your brothers and sisters in Christ.

• By responding "I do" to the third vow, you are confessing that you believe Jesus is the Son of God, came to earth to die for your sins, and by his death and resurrection has shown his love for you and forgiven your sins. You are promising to let Jesus determine how you live your life.

These are some pretty big commitments. We are going to take a few minutes now to look at a person from the Bible who, while not in these exact words, felt the assurance of Jesus' love and forgiveness so much that he was able to say "I do" to all three of those questions.

[Hand out copies of the "Big Faith" handout.]

SAY: I need three volunteers to read Luke 19:1-10 from the handout. After each person reads, I'll ask you to identify various ways that Zacchaeus made his profession of faith.

[Ask the students to follow the instructions on the handout. They are to complete certain actions after each reading of Luke 19:1-10. NOTE: The use of the "church language" or technical jargon on the handout is intentional to allow the students to become comfortable hearing the words that will be used during the confirmation service. Be prepared to explain again what these terms mean, referencing either the explanation above or your own words.]

Discussion Questions

- Do you think that John Wesley would have answered "I do" to these three questions before May 24, 1738? Why, or why not?

- Do you think Zacchaeus would have answered "I do" to these three questions before coming face to face with Jesus? Why, or why not?

- How did Zacchaeus make trusting Jesus look easy?

- What worldly things did Zacchaeus have to turn away from in order to serve Jesus?

- What do you think is the hardest thing about following Jesus?

- R E F L E C T -

Saying 'I Do' *5 minutes*

SAY: Now turn to your Student Guide and journal your answers to the questions in the Reflect section.

[Have students follow instructions and answer the questions.]

- CREATE -

What Was He Thinking? *15 minutes*

SAY: Who'd be willing to read aloud the instructions for the Create activity in your Student Guide?

[Ask the volunteer to read the instructions.]

SAY: Take about 10 minutes to complete this activity. Go!

[Allow time for the students to work on their own.]

SAY: Let's come back together and share our creations.

Discussion Questions *As Time Allows*

• Who'd like to share what you have created?

• What did you like about this activity? What was challenging?

• How did our lesson today inspire you to think or live differently?

- NEXT -

Ideas to Try This Week

[Point out the ideas to try during the week.]

At home: Write an online message to someone in your family who is an example of what it means to follow Jesus. Thank that person for the example he or she sets, and ask him or her how you can be encouraged to continue following Jesus more and more in your daily life.

At school: Find a friend and commit to sending each other text messages throughout the day, encouraging each other to follow Jesus during the school day.

In your community: Write a letter (yes, the old-fashioned kind with a pen and paper) to someone from your church community whose faith inspires you. Tell that person how his or her faith has had an impact on yours.

Confirm Teaching Plans

BIG FAITH

LUKE 19:1-10

[1] Jesus entered Jericho and was passing through town. [2] A man there named Zacchaeus, a ruler among tax collectors, was rich. [3] He was trying to see who Jesus was, but, being a short man, he couldn't because of the crowd. [4] So he ran ahead and climbed up a sycamore tree so he could see Jesus, who was about to pass that way. [5] When Jesus came to that spot, he looked up and said, "Zacchaeus, come down at once. I must stay in your home today." [6] So Zacchaeus came down at once, happy to welcome Jesus.

[7] Everyone who saw this grumbled, saying, "He has gone to be the guest of a sinner."

[8] Zacchaeus stopped and said to the Lord, "Look, Lord, I give half of my possessions to the poor. And if I have cheated anyone, I repay them four times as much."

[9] Jesus said to him, "Today, salvation has come to this household because he too is a son of Abraham. [10] The Human One came to seek and save the lost."

AFTER THE FIRST READING: Underline the ways Zacchaeus renounces wickedness, rejects evil, or repents of his sin.

AFTER THE SECOND READING: Circle examples of ways Zacchaeus commits to resist evil, injustice, or oppression.

AFTER THE THIRD READING: Create a list (below) of ways that Zacchaeus trusts in Jesus, promises to serve Jesus, and experiences the assurance that Jesus will forgive him of all his sins.

Lesson
35 A Faith to Live

LESSON DESCRIPTION: This lesson will help students explore Wesley's understanding of Christian perfection as it relates to living a life of following Christ. Using Matthew 22 as a guide, students will be encouraged to follow Jesus' way of life as Christians, using the Wesleyan practices of means of grace—works of piety and works of mercy—as ways to attain Christian perfection.

Lesson Outline

SECTION	TOPIC	DURATION
Connect	This Is Perfect	15 minutes
Explore	Piety or Mercy?	20 minutes
Reflect	Works for the World	10 minutes
Create	It's Off to Work We Go	15 minutes
Next	At home, at school, and in your community	Ideas to try this week

Supply List

Connect: This Is Perfect
- [ ] Current magazines to be cut apart
- [ ] Construction paper
- [ ] Scissors
- [ ] Glue
- [ ] Writing utensils
- [ ] Dry-erase board or flip chart
- [ ] Writing utensils

Explore: Piety or Mercy?
- [ ] "Piety" or "Mercy" signs
- [ ] Tape
- [ ] Student Guide (for leader reference)
- [ ] Paper (8.5 by 11)

Reflect: Works for the World
- [ ] Student Guides
- [ ] Writing utensils

Create: It's Off to Work We Go
- [ ] Student Guides
- [ ] Writing utensils

Next
- [ ] Student Guides

Confirm Teaching Plans

- C O N N E C T -

This Is Perfect *15 minutes*

[Bring in several magazines featuring current events and people (*People, Sports Illustrated, Seventeen, Vogue/Teen Vogue,* and so on.)]

SAY: Today we are going to be talking about living out our faith. We're going to start with thinking about perfection. You'll have 3 minutes to look through these magazines and find a picture that you think expresses perfection. The picture can be of someone who performs perfectly or looks perfect, of something that is perfect, or of somewhere that is perfect. Cut out this picture and glue it to the middle of a piece of paper.

[Allow time for everyone to make a selection and glue it to the paper.]

SAY: Now you are going to pass your paper to the person on your right. On the piece of paper you receive, write a word or phrase describing how the perfection in the picture is attained. Try not to repeat words if at all possible. For example, you might have a picture of a perfect wedding cake, and around that wedding cake could be words such as *practice, baking classes, lots of time, expensive kitchen gadgets, talented baker*.

When your picture gets back to you, circle the top 2 words or phrases that you think best describe how perfection is attained in your picture. Each person will share his or her top 2 words and I'll make a list so everyone can see it.

[Write the list of ways to attain perfection on the board or a flip chart and keep them up through the duration of the session.]

Discussion Questions

• Do you think that perfection is something that can be achieved? Why, or why not?

• Why is perfection so enticing to some people?

• What are people willing to do or be or give up to strive for perfection?

SAY: John Wesley thought and taught that Christian perfection was attainable. Seems kind of a daunting task for humans to be perfect. As we start talking about Christian perfection, keep in mind this list of our top ways to attain perfection.

- EXPLORE -

Piety or Mercy? *20 minutes*

[**LEADER PREP:** Create 2 signs: one labeled "Works of Piety: Connecting With God" and the other "Works of Mercy: Caring for Others." Designate one side of the room as the piety side and the other side of the room as the mercy side, and put up the corresponding signs. Write each work of Piety and Mercy (listed on the chart in the Reflect section of the Student Guide) on an 8.5-by-11 sheet of paper.]

SAY: In a writing that took several years to compile John Wesley answers the question "What is Christian perfection?" this way, "The loving [of] God with all our heart, mind, soul, and strength. This implies that no wrong temper, none contrary to love, remains in the soul; and that all the thoughts, words, and actions are governed by pure love." For Wesley, being a "perfect Christian" meant fully loving God *and* your neighbor.

Wesley believed that the journey to Christian perfection was a lifelong journey. It was a process by which human beings could become more like Christ. Wesley didn't just say we should be "going on toward perfection"; he also gave people directions to grow toward Christian perfection. He called these directions "means of grace."

There are two categories of means of grace. First are works of piety (point to the sign), which are things we do that help us personally connect with God and prepare us to be God in the world. Second are works of mercy (point to the sign), which are things we do for others to let the world see God living in us. You can't do works of mercy without doing works of piety, and there's no point in doing works of piety if you're not going to follow it up with works of mercy.

We're going to play a little game to help us learn what is what. I am going to hand each of you a piece of paper. Please leave it face down until it's your turn.

Confirm Teaching Plans

[Hand out a "work" sign to each teen, until all the signs are distributed. This may mean that a teen receives more than one sign, or in large groups, that teens must gather into groups.]

SAY: Written on this piece of paper is either a work of piety or a work of mercy. That side of our room (*point*) is the piety side and that side of the room (*point*) is the mercy side. Each of you will take a turn reading your "works" sign aloud, and then you will have 5 seconds to place your sign on the table or floor on the correct side of the room. Everyone else will be shouting at you which side they think you should put it on. It will be up to you to decide where to put the sign. After all the signs are placed, I will tell you how many you have correct on each side. Who would like to begin? Remember, the group should shout out which side they think it should go on.

[After all of signs are placed, tell the students the number that are correct in each category, for example: "You have 5 of 9 correct in Works of Piety."]

SAY: Now, you have 1 minute to switch as many signs as you wish to try and get them in the correct categories. Work together!

[After all signs are properly categorized, tape them around the poster.]

SAY: Remember, we said earlier that Wesley believed that Christian perfection was "The loving [of] God with all our heart, mind, soul, and strength...so that all the thoughts, words, and actions are governed by pure love." He didn't come up with this on his own—this was a teaching that had been part of the Hebrew tradition, which Jesus Christ drew and expanded upon.

I need volunteers to read Deuteronomy 6:4-6 and Matthew 22:36-40.

[Ask the volunteers to read the Scriptures aloud.]

Discussion Questions

- How did Jesus modify the Great Commandment in Deuteronomy to the Greatest Commandment in Matthew?

- Look at the lists of works of piety—how can these actions or practices help you "love the Lord with all your heart, all your being, and all your mind"?

- Look at the list of works of mercy—how can these actions and practices help you "love their neighbor as yourself"?

- How could structuring our lives around these means of grace eventually lead us to living a life guided by pure love, also known as a "perfect life"?

SAY: The journey to Christian perfection should not be understood as a way to make yourself better than others, or as an attempt to earn your way into heaven. We do not engage in the means of grace to prove to others how holy we are. This journey to Christian perfection is a response to the love that is given to you from God through Jesus' death and resurrection. It is how believers act on the grace that God gives us freely. It is how believers say to Jesus, "I see and accept the sacrifice you made for me, and I am going to constantly work on my life to make it look more like yours."

- R E F L E C T -

Works for the World 10 minutes

SAY: Now turn to the Reflect section in your Student Guide and consider which of these works of piety and mercy you already do that bring you closer to Christ, and which you might want to start doing to bring you closer to Christ..

[Give the students time to respond in their Student Guides.]

- C R E A T E -

It's Off to Work We Go 15 minutes

SAY: Who'd be willing to read aloud the instructions for the Create activity in your Student Guide?

[Ask the volunteer to read the instructions to the class.]

SAY: Take about 10 minutes to complete this activity. Go!

[Allow the students time to work on their own.]

SAY: Let's come back together and share our creations.

Confirm Teaching Plans

Discussion Questions *As Time Allows*

• Who would like to begin and share what you created?

• What did you like about this activity? What was challenging?

• How did our lesson today inspire you to think or live differently?

- N E X T -

Ideas to Try This Week

[Point out the ideas to try during the week.]

At home: Choose one act of piety and one act of mercy that you want to intentionally practice this week at home. Make sure you do them both at least once each day.

At school: Talk with your friends about how you can care for others at school. How do works of mercy impact your faith? How do they impact the world around you?

In your community: Talk with your pastor and visit someone from your church who is in the hospital or unable to leave home. Talk with this person about what you have been learning in confirmation class. Ask about the things he or she learned in church at your age.

Lesson 36 A Call to Follow

LESSON DESCRIPTION: Being called by God is a unique and critical portion of every Christian's journey. When Christ asks, "Will you follow me?" and you say yes, then Christ responds, "Here's how…" We can go astray on our journey when we take our eyes of God or ignore God's call. Exploring God's calling is an important part of accepting faith for oneself. This session will help students to know that God calls each person to work for God in special and specific ways. Sometimes the call is exciting and fun, sometimes the call is challenging and outside our comfort zone, but whatever the call we are responsible for following it.

Lesson Outline

SECTION	TOPIC	DURATION
Connect	Simon Says Meets Ro Sham Bo	15 minutes
Explore	A Tale of Two Calls	20 minutes
Reflect	Tuning in God	10 minutes
Create	Wanted: You	15 minutes
Next	At home, at school, and in your community	Ideas to try this week

Supply List

Connect: Simon Says Meets Ro Sham Bo
❑ List of your Simon Says actions already
   planned out

Explore: A Tale of Two Calls
❑ Scripture references to give to groups
❑ Paper
❑ Writing utensils
❑ Bibles
❑ Flip chart or dry-erase board
❑ Marker

Reflect: Tuning in God
❑ Student Guides
❑ Writing utensils

Create: Wanted: You
❑ Student Guides
❑ Writing utensils

Next
❑ Student Guides

IMPORTANT LESSON 39 PREP: In Lesson 39, you will need notes and letters from adults who have been supportive of students throughout the confirmation journey (teachers, mentors, parents, congregation member, pastor and other church staff). Ask them to write short notes or letters of affirmation and encouragement to the students. If the class is large, assign specific adults to specific teens. If the class is small, ask the adults to write a note to each teen. Send a reminder each week so that the notes and letters won't be rushed. Collect them in time to hand them out during the last lesson.

Confirm Teaching Plans

- C O N N E C T -

Simon Says Meets Ro Sham Bo *15 minutes*

[*LEADER PREP:* You may find it helpful to create a list of your Simon Says instructions prior to beginning the game. This may help to minimize the chaos you experience while leading this game.]

SAY: Today we're going to start with a mash-up game. We are going to play Simon Says and Rock, Paper, Scissors—called "Ro Sham Bo"—at the same time. Pay close attention to these rules, and during the game, because things are about to get chaotic and distracting.

STEP 1: Simon (me) will begin with some easy instructions. For example, I may say something like: "Simon says, pat your belly. Stop patting your belly." Any of you who stop patting your belly, would be considered "out" and now would be part of the Rock, Paper, Scissors game.

STEP 2A: Those now out of Simon Says must immediately begin to wander amongst the remaining Simon Says players calling out "Ro Sham Bo" until you find someone to play with. Then very loudly, you say "Rock, Paper, Scissors, Shoot" and throw your decided item. Remember rock smashes scissors, scissors cut paper, paper covers rock.

STEP 2B: The game of Simon Says will continue while the newly ousted members join the game of Ro Sham Bo. Those still in Simon Says will have to continue to pay attention to Simon's instructions. Simon's instructions will continue at the same volume, but will increase in difficulty as the game progresses.

STEP 3: The final two remaining Simon Says players will face off in an epic battle of rock, paper, scissors (best 2 out of 3) to determine the winner of the game.

[After the game, move on to the discussion questions.]

Discussion Questions

• What was it like to try to listen to Simon's instructions with other voices and activities going on around you?

• What was it like to be ignoring Simon's instructions while being intentionally distracting to other players?

Lesson 36

• What connections, if any, can you draw between this activity and trying to understand God's directions in your life?

SAY: Today we are going to talk about calling. To sense the calling that God has for our lives, we often have to listen and focus beyond the distractions around us. We have to slow down and pay attention to the ways in which God is revealing our purpose in and around us.

[Share your own experience of having answered a call from God in the midst of distractions, or of having followed a distraction rather than answering God's call.]

- E X P L O R E -

A Tale of Two Calls 20 minutes

SAY: We are going to break into groups of three or four people. Half of the groups will be assigned the character Saul, the other half Ananias.

[Assign half the groups Saul, giving them the associated Scripture references, and the other groups Ananias, again with associated Scripture references.]

If the group is not large enough to divide, prepare the monologue for Saul yourself prior to the session and use it as an example for the teens to follow. Have the entire group work together to develop the monologue for Ananias. Be sure to read Acts 9:1-9 and 17-22, so that the teens will hear the entire encounter.]

Saul — Acts 9:1-9, 17-22

Ananias — Acts 9:10-18

SAY: As a group you are going to take on the personality of your assigned Biblical figure. You are tasked to retell his story using his internal monologue. As a group you will go through the Scripture passage and reimagine what Saul or Ananias was thinking, feeling, and deciding throughout his encounter with God. As you're examining the story, be sure to imagine the

1. the emotions involved

2. the implications and potential ramifications of the call God is giving him

3. what made him ultimately agree to follow God's call

While the entire group will work on the script, each group will select one performer/reader. As a group, rewrite your person's encounter with God in 6 to 8 sentences. Have a writer record your retelling. The reader will then "perform" the monologue of their assigned person.

[After the performances, move on to the discussion.]

Discussion Questions

- What are the differences between Saul and Ananias? (Keep a list where everyone can see.)

- How were their calls different?

- How does God's call impact their lives differently?

- What could have happened to Saul if Ananias had ignored God's call?

- Who had the most to lose from following God's call?

- Do you know of other accounts in the Scriptures similar to this one? (Moses, Samuel)

SAY: There are many ways to talk about calling, because God's call to each person is different. However, we can break God's calling down into two basic categories. God has both a general and specific calling for each and every person. The general calling we *all* have is to follow Jesus and to be molded into living as he lived. This calling shapes how we view the world and our place in it.

Additionally, God gives us more specific callings. Sometimes our calling is like Saul's, ongoing, and involves a complete change in direction for our lives. We get called to a vocational direction or faithful cause and it becomes our focus for years. This kind of specific calling shapes how we spend our lives in service to God.

Other times we sense a calling for a specific moment or a season — this is an opportunity to step into God's story and play a role, like Ananias did. This kind of specific calling shapes how we show God's love to the world.

As we are all trying to live out God's general call of following the way of Jesus, we also need to be aware of how to recognize God's specific call for us. Discerning if God's call is for a moment, for a season, or for a long period of your life takes practice and time. This is just another example of how our faith is a journey with God.

The Bible gives us several examples, like Saul, of God having to use dramatic means to help people discern, or recognize, their calling. Your discernment may come by being blinded by light or hearing an audible voice. However, you may also recognize the call as a feeling that leads you somewhere you did not intend to go. God's call often is a specific "sense" we get, one that is usually confirmed in several different ways.

You may get a stirring inside for a specific cause; you may get a sense of direction from a conversation with a mentor; or you may find something in reading the Scriptures that stays with you.

I know this is mystical and maybe a little vague, but when we talk about our spiritual experiences, often they seem to be just beyond the words we use to describe them.

Discussion Questions

• Have any of you ever "sensed" or experienced God? How?

• Have you ever had someone tell you about a call they received from God? What kind of words or imagery did they use to explain why they did what they did?

• In what ways does God call people? How might God call people to things that seem ordinary?

- R E F L E C T -

Tuning in God 10 minutes

SAY: If you have never experienced a call from God, or are uncertain if you have, that is completely reasonable. We're going to spend a few minutes now exploring how we can become more attuned to God's calling. I would remind you of the importance of the means of grace, which we talked about last session, as a wonderful way to help you begin to sense God's calling.

There are some components of a call that might be particularly helpful for you to know as you are figuring out when, if, and how God is calling you. We'll explore them as steps, though they may not always happen sequentially. As I explain them, follow along in your Student Guide.

Confirm Teaching Plans

Step 1—Skills: These are the things that you're both naturally good at and that you develop over time. Right now you might be naturally good at making friends, and this could develop over time into you being able to coordinate large groups of people to do a specific task. God's call is going to use the skills that you already have or that you have that can be improved. If you are tone deaf, then God's not going to call you to lead a rock band; you don't have the skill necessary for that call.

Skills: When you begin to understand your skills and how to use them.

Now take about 30 seconds to list the things you are good at.

[Allow the students 30 seconds to make their lists.]

SAY: **Step 2—Excuses:** Once you've figured out some of your skills, you may be inclined to come up with excuses to prove that God's not calling you to use those skills for God's purpose. You will always be able to come up with reasons why you don't want to do something. Excuses are the first line of distractions that keep us from following God's instructions.

Excuses: A phase where you convince yourself you can't do something.

Now take about 30 seconds to list some of the reasons you have used to get out of using your skills.

[Allow the students 30 seconds to make their lists.]

SAY: **Step 3—Confirmation:** God's not just going to speak to you about your calling, God's also going to use the people around you to motivate you. God will open other people's eyes to your skills and put them in your life to help direct you.

Confirmation: God starts using other people and experiences to motivate you to respond.

Now take about 30 seconds to list some people who encourage you to discover and use your skills. What skills and passions are they noticing in you?

[Allow the students 30 seconds to make their lists.]

SAY: **Step 4—Desire:** There may be skills people tell you that you are good at, but those skills bring you nothing but dread. God's calling is not one of dread. God won't call you to be a doctor if you faint at the sight of blood. God's call will be challenging, but at the end of the challenges you will have an overwhelming sense of joy in your calling.

Lesson 36

Desire: A time when you realize that doing what you're good at brings you joy and God joy.

Now take about 30 seconds to think about a time when you used your skills to do something for someone else. What did you feel? What did the other person feel? What causes are you most passionate about?

[Allow the students 30 seconds to make their lists.]

SAY: **Step 5—Opportunity:** You will have chance after chance to use your skills for God's purpose. Even when you walk away from the chance, God will find a way to give you another one. God may be calling you to read Scripture in worship, but you ignore the announcement in the bulletin, and you tune out when your pastor asks for help, but you finally pay attention when your youth leader texts you the Scripture reference and asks for your help.

Opportunity: God gives you the time and space to do what you're good at for God.

Now take about 30 seconds to list three specific ways you could use your skills and passions for God.

[Allow the students 30 seconds to make their lists.]

- C R E A T E -

Wanted: You 15 minutes

SAY: Who'd be willing to read aloud the instructions aloud for the Create activity in your Student Guide?

[Ask the volunteer to read the instructions to the class.]

SAY: Take about 10 minutes to complete this activity. Go!

[Allow the students time to work on their own.]

SAY: Let's come back together and share our creations.

Confirm Teaching Plans

Discussion Questions *As Time Allows*

• Who would like to begin and share what you created?

• What did you like about this activity? What was challenging?

• How did our lesson today inspire you to think or live differently?

- N E X T -

Ideas to Try This Week

[Point out the ideas to try during the week.]

At home: Ask a family member whether he or she has ever felt led to do something out of the ordinary. Talk about how his or her decision affected others in the family. Ask whether he or she has ever considered what you might be led to do that is out of the ordinary.

At school: God's call to live for Christ is not something we add on to what we do. It is how we live our life every day. Consider the extracurricular activities you are already involved in related to your school (clubs, sports, ensembles, and so on). How might you be called to share God's love through those activities? Who in those groups might need to hear about God through you?

In your community: Saul (also called Paul) was called by God to serve the people outside his immediate circle. What do you think the world's greatest need is? How might God be calling you to meet that need outside of your immediate circle of church, home, and school?

Lesson
37 A Spirit to Find

LESSON DESCRIPTION: A large barrier for many Christians in living out their faith is understanding how exactly that is done. Knowing, being comfortable with, and utilizing one's spiritual gifts is a primary way that a follower of Christ can live her or his faith daily. One of the last steps of equipping our teens to make a choice, or to say "yes," to follow Christ is to show them how God has created them to be in service in the world. This session focuses solely on helping teens learn what their spiritual gifts are and how they can be used in the church and community.

Lesson Outline

SECTION	TOPIC	DURATION
Connect	Lesson 37 video: "A Spirit to Find"	5 minutes
	Talents vs. Gifts	10 minutes
Explore	Spiritual Gifts Inventory	30 minutes
Reflect	What Did I Get?	5 minutes
Create	Design-a-Ministry	15 minutes
Next	At home, at school, and in your community	Ideas to try this week

Supply List

Connect: Talents vs. Gifts
❑ Lesson 37 video: "A Spirit to Find"
❑ Talent and Gift index cards (6 cards prepared ahead of time)
❑ Globe and stick figure pictures

Explore: Spiritual Gifts Inventory
❑ Copies of the "Spiritual Gifts Inventory and Assessment" handout
❑ Poster or chart of spiritual gifts (prepared ahead of time)
❑ Calculators (Some students will have them on their phones.)

❑ Writing utensils
❑ Bibles

Reflect: What Did I Get?
❑ Student Guides
❑ Writing utensils

Create: Design-a-Ministry
❑ Student Guides
❑ Writing utensils

Next
❑ Student Guides

IMPORTANT LESSON 39 PREP: Touch base with the adults who have been asked to write short notes or letters of affirmation and encouragement to the students. (See Lesson 36 for the first mention of this.) Remind them of the deadline, which is before the final lesson, Lesson 39.

- C O N N E C T -

Video Time *5 minutes*

[**LEADER PREP:** Before this session, make copies of the "Spiritual Gifts Inventory" handout, including the assessment pages, and complete one for yourself. Become familiar with the 9 different gifts that are referred to in the inventory and the video.]

SAY: The last time we were together we talked about our calling and that God calls us to use our skills for God's purposes. Our skills or talents are the things that we are good at that help us connect to the world we live in. Spiritual gifts are not that different, but they serve a different purpose. Our spiritual gifts are the special skills we have that help us connect God to the world around us. The distinction between the two is a little fuzzy. So we're going to watch a video and then play a quick game to help us think more clearly about just how special spiritual gifts are.

[Show the Lesson 37 video: "A Spirit to Find."]

SAY: In a few minutes each of you is going to complete a spiritual gifts inventory. This will help you begin to determine how God has created you to make connections between God and those around you. But before we get there, we may need to clarify just a bit more the difference between talents and gifts.

Talents vs. Gifts *10 minutes*

[**LEADER PREP:** Write each talent and gift listed below on a separate index card. On one piece of paper draw a globe and on another draw a stick figure. (Or print out a globe and a stick person from the Internet. Don't use a photo of a person because it is necessary to avoid applying a sex or ethnicity to the human figure.) Place the pictures on opposite sides of the room.]

Talents
- I have the highest batting average on our team.
- I have written code that helps keep cell phones from getting hacked.
- I never forget someone's name.

Gifts
- I never forget to give presents to my loved ones on their birthdays.
- I am always in the middle trying to stop a fight between friends.
- I constantly remind my siblings of their schedules and activities.

Lesson 37

[Give each index card to each student. Don't worry if there isn't a card for every student. This is supposed to be a quick activity.]

SAY: For those who have an index card, I would like you to stand one at a time and read your card so that everyone can hear you. Those sitting, you will yell out either "talent" or "gift" after the statement is read. The majority of opinion will determine which direction each person moves. If your statement is considered a talent, then you will move to the picture of the globe. If your statement is considered a gift, then you will move to the picture of the person. Stay there until all six skill and gift cards have been read.

[Once everyone has been categorized, either talent or gift, correct any incorrectly categorized people, then ask them to read their statements again.]

Discussion Questions

• What commonalities do you seen between the statements referring to people's gifts?

• How might any of these gifts be used as a way to connect with God?

SAY: We are now going to take a few minutes to explore what the Bible has to say about the gifts God has given humanity and why God gave them to us.

- E X P L O R E -

Spiritual Gifts Inventory 30 minutes

[**LEADER PREP:** Make a copy of the Spiritual Gift Inventory handout for each student. On a board or posterboard(s) make a chart by listing in a single column the spiritual gifts below. Entitle that column "Spiritual Gifts." Entitle a second, narrower column, "Rank." Keep this Spiritual Gifts Chart covered until later in this activity.]

Organizer / Leader
Caregiver / Shepherd
Planner / Visionary
Initiator / Catalyst
Worker / Helper

Confirm Teaching Plans

Encourager / Healer
Advisor / Discerner
Teacher / Mentor
Advocate / Prophet

SAY: You are now going to spend some time finding out what your spiritual gifts are. I am going to give each of you a Spiritual Gifts Inventory. There are 45 statements, and you will need to write beside each statement a number 0–3 representing how appropriately that statement describes you. There are instructions on the top of the inventory explaining what each number means. Take 5 to 10 seconds per statement to answer. Write down the first number that comes to your mind; do not try to think what the answer "should be" or what others would expect you to answer. This will only be as accurate as you are honest with yourself. Please take a minute to read over the instructions before you begin.

[Give each student a copy of the "Spiritual Gifts Inventory" handout and a writing utensil.]

Before you begin, I would like to offer a prayer for guidance for all of you. Let us pray:

God, we are here getting ready to figure out what special gifts you have given each of us. Send your Holy Spirit into our hearts and minds and help us to be open and honest with ourselves and with you. Help us understand the questions and what our answers should be. We ask this in the name of Jesus. Amen.

[Allow 10–15 minutes for the teens to complete the survey. After about 7 minutes, or once it appears that most of the students have completed the survey, provide the following instructions.]

SAY: Once you have completed the survey, you will need to compile your numbers. At the end of the survey you will find categories, and under each category are lists of numbers. In the blank beside the number on this answer sheet, write down the numerical ranking you recorded beside the corresponding number in the survey. Add all the ranking numbers in each category to get a total for each category. When you've gotten all your totals, circle your top 3 highest categories.

[Allow about 5 minutes for the students to compile their results. As the students are compiling results, uncover (or display) the Spiritual Gifts Chart you created before the session started. Once it appears that most teens have compiled their results, speak again.]

SAY: In the video we watched at the beginning of the session, we learned that there are many different spiritual gifts listed in Scripture. I would like 3 volunteers to read the different passages where Paul mentions spiritual gifts: Romans 12:4-8; Ephesians 4:11-13; and 1 Corinthians 12:4-11.

[Let the volunteers read the passages.]

SAY: Those passages point to a variety of gifts, but the survey you just took condenses them down to 9. This gives us a more focused direction for seeing how God wants us to be at work in the world. We can learn a lot about each other and where God may be calling this group to lead by seeing how we are all gifted. I'm going to ask all of you to come up and put a 1, 2, and 3 in the rank category beside your top 3 spiritual gifts so that we can get a sense of what gifts are present in our group and which, if any, are missing.

[Allow the students to mark their gifts on the chart.]

Discussion Questions

• What gifts do we share? How can that be helpful in serving God together?

• How can we support our sisters and brothers who have gifts others don't share? How can having those unique individuals be helpful in serving God together?

• Were there any gifts mentioned in the Scripture passages that you wish had been on the survey?

- R E F L E C T -

What Did I Get? 5 minutes

SAY: Now turn to your Student Guide and journal a response to the questions there.

[Give the students 2 minutes to answer the questions in the Student Guide. Then ask for a couple volunteers to share their responses to those questions:]

• What are the top three spiritual gifts that you connected with?

• How have you already seen God using these gifts in your life?

- C R E A T E -

Design-a-Ministry *15 minutes*

SAY: Who'd be willing to read aloud the instructions aloud for the Create activity in your Student Guide?

[Ask the volunteer to read the instructions.]

SAY: Take about 10 minutes to complete this activity. Go!

[Allow the students time to work on their own.]

SAY: Let's come back together and share our creations.

Discussion Questions *As Time Allows*

• Who'd like to share what you have created?

• What did you like about this activity? What was challenging?

• How did our lesson today inspire you to think or live differently?

- N E X T -

Ideas to Try This Week

[Point out the ideas to try during the week.]

At home: Find out the spiritual gifts of the others in your home. Compare the gifts God has given each person. Create a plan for how each of you could use your gifts at home to serve one another and make the family stronger.

At school: Ask a few of your friends what they think you are good at and compare their answers to the spiritual gifts that you have. What do your friends see about you that you don't see? How are you using your spiritual gifts as a witness to God's presence in your life?

In your community: Part of the importance of knowing your spiritual gifts is that it helps you use them to affect the world around you for the glory of God. Write down one way you can affect your neighborhood using each of your top three spiritual gifts. Try to do these actions during the week.

SPIRITUAL GIFTS INVENTORY

God has blessed all of us with many gifts and talents. God calls us to use all of these talents in service of God and others. But the Holy Spirit has also blessed us with spiritual gifts. Complete this survey to get a sense of the spiritual gifts the Spirit has given you.

For each of the following statements, indicate how true the statement is for you, using one of the following numbers:

3—yes, all the time
2—yes, sometimes
1—maybe, occasionally
0—no, never

___ 1. When it comes to schoolwork and extra-curricular activities, I am organized and focused on the details.

___ 2. I keep up with news about people who are hurting in my community and/or around the world.

___ 3. I am a good listener who is patient with friends who need someone to talk to.

___ 4. Before I say yes to anything, I make sure that it is consistent with my Christian faith.

___ 5. I love learning all that I can about the Bible and Christian beliefs and traditions.

___ 6. I feel deep sadness when I hear about people in other parts of the world who are hurting.

___ 7. I am eager to participate in hands-on service projects and to go on mission trips.

___ 8. When I see a problem or injustice in my community I speak out.

___ 9. When I see something that needs to be done, I do it without being asked.

___ 10. I keep track of events and activities on a planner or calendar and am always aware of what I have scheduled and what responsibilities I have.

___ 11. I know that I don't have all the answers and am eager to hear what others have to say.

___ 12. I see God at work in the lives of others.

___ 13. I am eager to use my gifts and talents in new ways.

___ 14. I am a hard worker who doesn't stop until the project I'm working on is finished.

___ 15. I make a point of encouraging my friends and peers by attending their games, performances, and ceremonies.

___ 16. I keep my faith in mind when choosing movies to watch and music to listen to.

___ 17. I'm eager to help friends and classmates with schoolwork.

___ 18. I am comfortable telling other people about my faith.

___ 19. I'm always looking for ways to draw attention to things that I care about.

___ 20. I am good at explaining things through speaking and/or writing.

___ 21. Before I post anything on the Internet, I stop to think about how the words or pictures I post reflect my Christian faith.

1

___ 22. When a friend is absent from school or church, I call to check on him or her.

___ 23. I am good at building things and putting things together.

___ 24. When something needs to be done, I prefer to get to work right away, without spending much time planning and organizing.

___ 25. When I see something beautiful or incredible in the natural world, I think of God, the Creator.

___ 26. I like to know all the facts about an issue or situation before forming an opinion.

___ 27. I enjoy planning and organizing events at school and at church.

___ 28. I am comfortable in leadership roles.

___ 29. When there is an argument or a dispute, I always listen to all sides of the story.

___ 30. At school and church, I notice people who are lonely or sad and people who are absent.

___ 31. I am willing (and eager) to go anywhere in the world to do God's work.

___ 32. In school, I prefer assignments that involve working with my hands to assignments that simply involve reading and writing.

___ 33. I go out of my way to celebrate with friends who have reached a milestone or achieved something important, and I go out of my way to console friends who are having a tough time.

___ 34. I use what I know of the Bible and the teaching of the church whenever I have to make a difficult decision.

___ 35. I love telling others about interesting new things I have learned.

___ 36. I am comfortable speaking to a large group of people.

___ 37. Before I start on a project or task, I figure out exactly what steps I need to take and make a plan.

___ 38. I listen carefully to my teachers and pastors and am eager to learn from what they say.

___ 39. I'm observant and tend to notice things that many other people overlook.

___ 40. I pay attention to and spend time with people who are lonely and sad.

___ 41. I am careful about whom I hang out with so that I don't end up in dangerous situations or situations where I will be tempted to do something I know is wrong.

___ 42. I can explain complicated ideas so that they're easy for people to understand.

___ 43. I like to use my gifts and talents to tell people about God and to make people aware of those who are suffering from illness, hunger, poverty, or disasters.

___ 44. I'm willing to drop anything and everything to help a friend in need.

___ 45. I don't mind getting dirty for a good cause.

2

SPIRITUAL GIFTS ASSESSMENT

Fill in your answers to the Spiritual Gifts Inventory (pages 1–2) in the appropriate spaces below. Then add up the numbers to determine which best describe(s) your spiritual gifts. Some people may be especially gifted in one or two ways; others may be moderately gifted in many ways. Regardless of how we are gifted, all of us are blessed and called to serve God and others as parts of Christ's body.

ORGANIZER / LEADER
You are organized and have natural leadership abilities. When something needs to be done, you prefer to make a plan and see it through, step by step.

1. _____ 10. _____ 27. _____ 28. _____ 37. _____ Total: _____

CAREGIVER / SHEPHERD
You are a good listener. You listen to friends who are hurting, pay attention to teachers and pastors, and hear the cries of those who are in need.

3. _____ 11. _____ 26. _____ 29. _____ 38. _____ Total: _____

PLANNER / VISIONARY
You see all the ways that God is at work in the world around you and have an eye for the work that God is calling Christians to do.

2. _____ 12. _____ 25. _____ 30. _____ 39. _____ Total: _____

INITIATOR / CATALYST
You are quick to respond and go wherever you need to go to do the work God has called you to do.

9. _____ 13. _____ 24. _____ 31. _____ 44. _____ Total: _____

WORKER / HELPER
You are a hard worker and aren't afraid to get your hands dirty doing work that needs to be done.

7. _____ 14. _____ 23. _____ 32. _____ 45. _____ Total: _____

ENCOURAGER / HEALER
You are compassionate and sympathize with the pain that others are feeling. You encourage your friends and peers in times of celebration and in times of sadness.

6. _____ 15. _____ 22. _____ 33. _____ 40. _____ Total: _____

3

ADVISOR / DISCERNER

You are the filter. You know what things are healthy for the body of Christ and what things are not. You embrace what is good and stay away from what is bad.

4. _____ 16. _____ 21. _____ 34. _____ 41. _____ Total: _____

TEACHER / MENTOR

You understand complex ideas and processes and are able to explain them to others in ways that make sense.

5. _____ 17. _____ 20. _____ 35. _____ 42. _____ Total: _____

ADVOCATE / PROPHET

You speak truth, taking a stand against injustice and proclaiming the good news of Christ. You don't hesitate to tell people what they need to hear.

8. _____ 18. _____ 19. _____ 36. _____ 43. _____ Total: _____

Lesson
38 A Story to Tell

LESSON DESCRIPTION: A key component of the Christian journey is being able and willing to share your faith experiences with others. For many, this is one of the hardest parts of being a Christian and therefore one of the most neglected spiritual and evangelistic practices. The confirmation journey should be full of a multitude of opportunities for teens to encounter God in a variety of ways. Being able to recognize that one has encountered God and being able to articulate those encounters are important skills for teens to develop. This next to last session will give teens a variety of opportunities to share stories from their time in confirmation class as practice for sharing their faith with others outside confirmation. More important, they will be given an opportunity to write out what it is they have come to believe as a Christian through this confirmation journey.

Lesson Outline

SECTION	TOPIC	DURATION
Connect	Grab Bag Storytelling	15 minutes
Explore	What Just Happened There?	25 minutes
Reflect	A Story to Tell	5 minutes
Create	I Believe	15 minutes
Next	At home, at school, and in your community	Ideas to try this week

Supply List

Connect: Grab Bag Storytelling
❏ Journey items (examples: water bottle, map, compass, sunglasses, adhesive bandages, snack food, toothbrush, phone charger)
❏ Bag for journey items

Explore: What Just Happened There?
❏ Dry-erase board or posterboard
❏ Marker

Reflect: A Story to Tell
❏ Student Guides
❏ Writing utensils

Create: I Believe
❏ Student Guides
❏ Writing utensils

Next
❏ Student Guides

IMPORTANT LESSON 39 PREP: Touch base with the adults who have been asked to write short notes or letters of affirmation and encouragement to the students. (See Lesson 36 for the first mention of this.) Remind them of the deadline, which is before the final lesson, Lesson 39.

- C O N N E C T -

Grab Bag Storytelling *15 minutes*

[**LEADER PREP:** Before the lesson, gather an assortment of items you would associate with taking a journey and put them all in a bag. Items could include: water bottle, map, compass, sunglasses, adhesive bandages, snack foods, toothbrush, phone charger, and so forth. Make sure you have one item for each teen in your group.]

SAY: I'm going to ask each of you to select one item from this bag as I walk around. You are not to look in the bag while you are reaching in, and you must grab the first thing that you touch. Once everyone has an item, I will explain what we are going to do with them. You will not be able to switch items.

[Allow each student to reach into the bag and grab an item without looking or feeling around.]

SAY: Now that everyone has an item, each of you is going to use your item as inspiration for telling a story about your confirmation journey. If you cannot come up with a way to link your item with your confirmation journey, then share a story from your life that relates to that item.

I will start. I'll use my cellphone as an example. My cell phone reminds me of that time when . . . .

[Tell your story. Then allow everyone an opportunity to share his or her story or to pass.]

SAY: The people, places, and things we encounter on our journeys have an interesting way of impacting how we remember what took place and the reason we tell others what took place. It's important that we hear one another's stories and understand how we experience our journeys with God differently, because in hearing how others experience God, we are better able to explain how we experience God. Sharing our stories strengthens the Body of Christ and is an important component of being a follower of Christ. We're going to take some time now to explore how sharing stories from our lives is part of what it means to be a follower of Christ.

- EXPLORE -

What Just Happened There? 25 minutes

SAY: Have you ever been in a situation where you've had to ask the question, "What just happened there?" Maybe you were in class and you zoned out for a bit, and you leaned over to a friend to find out what you missed. Maybe you were watching a sports event where you weren't familiar with the rules and you had to ask someone to clarify why the player was being escorted out of the game. Or maybe you were with a group of people and something so amazing happened that you couldn't process the entire meaning of it and you needed to hear their perspective to totally understand what was going on.

The Gospel of Luke has a detailed description of an encounter Cleopas and another disciple had with the risen Christ. In this one description, Luke writes about three different stories. The first story is how the disciples remembered and experienced the life, death, and resurrection of Jesus. The second story is how Jesus explained and taught these traveling disciples about all of the Scriptures in light of his life, death, and resurrection. The third story is of how Cleopas and the other disciple couldn't keep this encounter with the Risen Christ to themselves. We are going to go through this encounter with Jesus one story at a time, and think together about "What just happened there"?

I need three volunteers: one to read Luke 24:13-24, the next to read continue reading verses 25-27, and the last to continue reading with verses 28-35. After each reader, we are going to stop and talk about "what just happened there."

> [As the first reader reads Luke 24:13-24, write "Cleopas and the other disciple" on a dry-erase board or on pieces of posterboard. When the reader is done, write down under that heading the students' answers to the following questions:

Discussion Questions

• What did Cleopas report had just happened in Jerusalem?

• What, do you think, was Cleopas's intention for telling this stranger about what had just happened in Jerusalem? Why did he do it?

- If Cleopas had not been telling these events to Jesus and had, in fact, been talking to a stranger who didn't know Jesus, how, do you think, would that person have reacted to the story?

  [As the second reader reads Luke 24:25-27, underneath the students' answers to the previous questions, write "Jesus." When the reader is done, write down under that heading the students' answers to the following questions:]

Discussion Questions

- What did Jesus explain to Cleopas and the other traveler had just happened in Jerusalem?

- What do you think was Jesus' intention in telling these two about what had just happened in Jerusalem? Why did he do it?

- If the travelers had known it was Jesus explaining the Scriptures to them, how do you think they would have reacted differently to the story they had been told?

  [As the third reader reads Luke 24:28-35, underneath the teens answers to the previous questions, write "Cleopas and the other disciple." When the reader is done, write down under that heading the teens' answers to the following questions:]

- What did the two traveling disciples report had just happened on the way to Emmaus?

- What do you think was their intention in telling the other disciples in Jerusalem about what had just happened to them? Why did they do it?

- If the traveling disciples had not known the disciples in Jerusalem, who do you think they would have told about this encounter they had with the risen Christ?

  [Direct the students' attention to the board as they answer the following questions:]

- What are the different reasons for telling each of these stories?

- Do you think that the reason for telling the story affected what information the storyteller relayed and how he relayed it? Why, or why not?

Lesson 38

- What are the reasons we tell others about our faith experiences or encounters with God?

- How might knowing the reason we share our faith experiences or encounters with God affect who we share the story with and what we tell them?

- Why is hearing stories about things that have happened directly to someone more exciting than reading stories about things happening to other people?

- How, do you think, is God involved when we tell stories about our faith experiences? (Consider how God was involved in each part of each story in this passage from Luke.)

SAY: There are many different things we can learn about sharing stories from the Road to Emmaus story. We learn from the traveling disciples that you never know who you're talking to or what kind of story you're going to end up with at the end of the day. We learn from Jesus that God plays a significant role in the story of our lives. We also learn that as we share stories, God continues to be present and active in the world.

Luke 24:35 says, "Then the two disciples described what had happened along the road and how Jesus was made known to them as he broke the bread." These disciples were on a journey. Along that journey they felt a variety of emotions; they told someone about the events in their lives that were concerning them; they listened as someone helped them understand the importance of Scripture to their present situation; they invited a stranger to stay with them; and they ate together.

Then they had an experience with the risen Christ, and that experience changed their story. Where just hours before they had "downcast faces" they all of a sudden had a new hope and people to share it with. They didn't have this powerful experience and keep it to themselves. They immediately went to find people to share their experience with. Their acceptance that Jesus is alive was not the end of the journey, but just the beginning.

It may seem like this journey of confirmation is coming to an end. You've felt a variety of emotions, you've shared with others where you are in life, you've listened as other people of faith have explained how God's word shapes how we live, you've hung in this journey together, and goodness knows you've eaten. Somewhere along the way, you have experienced God. And just like the disciples on the road to Emmaus, you can't keep that experience to yourself.

- R E F L E C T -

A Story to Tell *5 minutes*

SAY: Now turn to your Student Guide and follow the directions in the Reflect section.

[Give the students time to respond in their Student Guides.]

SAY: Sharing our holy experiences can be scary. Practice makes it easier to do. Share your answer with one other person in the room.

- C R E A T E -

I Believe *15 minutes*

SAY: Who'd be willing to read aloud the instructions aloud for the Create activity in your Student Guide?

[Ask the volunteer to read the instructions to the class.]

SAY: Take about 10 minutes to complete this activity. Go!

[Allow the students time to work on their own.]

SAY: Let's come back together and share our creations.

Discussion Questions *As Time Allows*

• Who would like to begin and share what you created?

• What did you like about this activity? What was challenging?

• How did our lesson today inspire you to think or live differently?

- N E X T -

Ideas to Try This Week

[Point out the ideas to try during the week.]

At home: Find a quiet place at home and read the letter you wrote at the beginning of your confirmation journey. How have you changed? Who do you want to tell? What will you say to them?

At school: Tell a friend at school about your confirmation journey. Invite him or her to come to the confirmation worship service and sit with your family.

In your community: God is with people even when they don't recognize it. Where do you see God in your community? How can you help others to recognize God is with them? What can you tell them about your confirmation journey as an example?

Lesson

39 A Journey to Continue

LESSON DESCRIPTION: This final lesson is an opportunity for the students to lift one another up and surround one another in Christian love. Hopefully, the support they feel from their peers will be encouraging for them to take the next step toward confirmation. The students will also be challenged to create an action plan for their next steps in the Christian journey. These steps will not be dependent upon being confirmed but will be commitments to continued growth and discipleship.

Lesson Outline		
SECTION	TOPIC	DURATION
Connect	Where Are You Now?	10 minutes
Explore	Group and Individual Affirmations	35 minutes
Reflect	Affirmation Exploration	5 minutes
Create	Looking Back, Looking Forward	15 minutes
Next	At home, at school, and in your community	Ideas to try this week

Supply List

Connect: Where Are You Now?
❏ Copies of the "Where Are You Now?" questionnaire (in Lesson 4)
❏ Completed "Where Are You Now?" questionnaires from Lesson 4
❏ Writing utensils

Explore: Group and Individual Affirmations
❏ Copies of the "Group Affirmation" handout
❏ Copies of the "Affirmation Cards"
❏ Copies of the "Blank Cards"
❏ Paper bags (one per student)
❏ Items to decorate with (stickers, markers, glitter, glue, and so forth)
❏ Writing utensils

Reflect: Affirmation Exploration
❏ Student Guides
❏ Writing utensils

Create: Looking Back, Looking Forward
❏ Student Guides
❏ Writing utensils
❏ Letters of affirmation from adults (first mentioned in Lesson 36, on the bottom of page 240)

Next
❏ Student Guides

- C O N N E C T -

Where Are You Now? *10 minutes*

[**LEADER PREP:** If you have not already done so (see opening page of Lessons 36–38), reach out to adults that have been supportive of students throughout the confirmation journey (teachers, mentors, parents, congregation members, pastor and other church staff) and ask them to write short notes or letters of affirmation and encouragement to the students. If the class is large, assign specific adults to specific teens. If the class is small, ask the adults to write a note to each teen. You will give the students these letters of affirmation at the end of the lesson. Make copies of the "Where Are You Now?" questionnaire.]

SAY: We started this journey together by surveying how we felt about confirmation. It's important for us to take a few minutes to see where we've come along this journey. We wrote letters to ourselves, and if you didn't take the opportunity to read that before coming in today, I highly recommend that you do that. Now, you're going to re-survey yourself and we're going to talk together about how things have changed during this experience.

[Give each student a copy of the "Where Are You Now?" questionnaire and have the students fill them out. After a few minutes, hand out the questionnaires that they filled out in Lesson 4.]

Discussion Questions

• Without giving specific numbers, were there any of these questions where you experienced a change from the first time you took this? What, do you think, led to that change?

• What is one thing that you wish you had known or better understood at the beginning of this journey?

• What is something that you now understand better as a result of taking this journey?

• Who do you know that would benefit from taking this journey (kid, teen, or adult)?

SAY: As we end our time together as this confirmation community, it's important that we not only remember where we started but also lift up and support one another in the changes we have seen. We are going to experience two different types of affirmations today. In the Christian context, affirmations are ways we say to one another, "I see God in you." We are offering more than a pat on the back to a friend or a generic comment in a yearbook, or a heart on Instagram. An affirmation is a way to encourage one another to stay strong in God and keep going when times get tough.

- E X P L O R E -

Group and Individual Affirmations 35 minutes

[**LEADER PREP:** Make copies of the "Group Affirmation" Litany is on the bottom of the survey handout for this lesson. This litany could also be used during the confirmation worship service liturgy. Make multiple copies of the "Affirmation Cards" and cut them apart. Stack each different statement in its own deck. If possible, print them onto cardstock or heavy paper. Be sure also to include a deck of blank cards for anyone who wants to create his or her own affirmation.]

SAY: Who'd be willing to read Ephesians 2:14-22 for us?

[Ask the volunteer to read.]

SAY: Paul is affirming the great work of Jesus as he brought together people who were once separate and strangers to create this great community of love and support. Paul is also affirming the people who have accepted Jesus' invitation to be a part of this community and encouraging them to remember what was done for them and live a life according to that gift.

Let's join together in a group affirmation from the Scripture we just heard, Ephesians 2:14-22.

[Lead the students in reading the "Group Affirmation" litany.]

SAY: Thank you for joining together in that group affirmation. I'm going to hand each of you a bag, and would like you to put your name on it and spend a couple minutes decorating it as you like.

[Hand out paper bags and decorating items. Ask the students to write their names on the bags and decorate them however they'd like.]

SAY: You have created a nice bag for yourself. Now others are going to fill your bag with affirmations and supportive comments. I have made 4 different affirmation cards and have them in piles here. You may select one of any of these cards for each person in our group. If you would like to create your own affirmation, without a prompt, there are also blank cards. Spend the next several minutes selecting and filling out a card for each person in our group. Your affirmations may be anonymous if you'd like.

[Allow time for students to complete the cards. Once everyone has distributed these cards, allow time for students to read through some of the cards in their bags.]

- R E F L E C T -

Affirmation Exploration *5 minutes*

SAY: Now that you've had time to support one another and feel supported, I'm going to give you a couple minutes to reflect on that process. The Reflect section of your Student Guide has some reflection questions to respond to. Please take a few minutes to think about and respond to those questions.

The following questions are from the Student Guide:

• What affirmation surprised you most? Why?

• How do these affirmations make you feel about being a part of a Christian community?

• How does giving others affirmations make you feel?

• How does this activity strengthen your faith?

- C R E A T E -

Looking Back, Looking Forward *15 minutes*

SAY: Who'd be willing to read aloud the instructions for the Create activity in your Student Guide?

[Ask the volunteer to read the instructions.]

SAY: Take about 10 minutes to complete this activity. Go!

[Allow about 10 minutes for the students to work on their own.]

SAY: Let's come back together and share our creations.

Discussion Questions

• Who'd like to share what you created?

• What did you like about this activity? What was challenging?

• How did our lesson today inspire you to think or live differently?

[Give the students the letters of affirmation and encouragement that were written to them.]

- NEXT -

Ideas to Try This Week

[Point out the ideas to try during the week.]

At home: Find a quiet space in your house and read through the affirmation letters you received. What do these letters make you think and feel? How do they affect your decision to be a part of a faith community?

At school: Give a positive affirmation to someone who looks like he or she needs it. Don't make it about appearance or performance, but about his or her character or how he or she treated someone else.

In your community: There is plenty of negativity in the world around us, but Christians are a people of hope and love. Take a few minutes to look around your community this week and see the positive things happening. Be sure to point this out to others either in conversation or through social media. Be a voice of hope and love to your neighbors.

GROUP AFFIRMATION

LEADER: Christ is our peace. He made both Jews and Gentiles into one group.

STUDENTS: With his body, he broke down the barrier of hatred that divided us.

LEADER: He canceled the detailed rules of the Law so that he could create one new person out of the two groups, making peace.

STUDENTS: He reconciled them both as one body to God by the cross, which ended the hostility to God.

LEADER: When he came, he announced the good news of peace to you who were far away from God and to you who were near. We both have access to the Father through Christ by the one Spirit.

STUDENTS: So now we are no longer strangers and aliens. Rather, we are fellow citizens with God's people, and we belong to God's household.

LEADER: As God's household, you are built on the foundation of the apostles and prophets with Christ Jesus himself as the cornerstone. The whole building is joined together in him, and it grows up into a temple that is dedicated to the Lord.

STUDENTS: Christ is building us into a place where God lives through the Spirit.

GROUP AFFIRMATION

LEADER: Christ is our peace. He made both Jews and Gentiles into one group.

STUDENTS: With his body, he broke down the barrier of hatred that divided us.

LEADER: He canceled the detailed rules of the Law so that he could create one new person out of the two groups, making peace.

STUDENTS: He reconciled them both as one body to God by the cross, which ended the hostility to God.

LEADER: When he came, he announced the good news of peace to you who were far away from God and to you who were near. We both have access to the Father through Christ by the one Spirit.

STUDENTS: So now we are no longer strangers and aliens. Rather, we are fellow citizens with God's people, and we belong to God's household.

LEADER: As God's household, you are built on the foundation of the apostles and prophets with Christ Jesus himself as the cornerstone. The whole building is joined together in him, and it grows up into a temple that is dedicated to the Lord.

STUDENTS: Christ is building us into a place where God lives through the Spirit.

Permission is granted to the purchaser to photocopy this page for use with Confirm. *© 2010 Cokesbury.*

AFFIRMATION CARDS

I saw Christ working through you when . . .

When you said . . .

it helped me to better understand . . .

God has given you the gift of . . .

You have made my life better because . . .

BLANK CARDS